Political Obligation

LIBRARY OF POLITICAL STUDIES

GENERAL EDITOR:
PROFESSOR H. VICTOR WISEMAN

Department of Government
University of Exeter

Political Obligation

by Thomas McPherson

Senior Lecturer, Department of Philosophy
University College, Cardiff

LONDON

ROUTLEDGE & KEGAN PAUL

NEW YORK: HUMANITIES PRESS

First published 1967
by Routledge and Kegan Paul Ltd
Broadway House, 68-74 Carter Lane
London, E.C.4

Printed in Great Britain
by Willmer Brothers Limited
Birkenhead

© *Thomas McPherson 1967*

SBN 7100 5121 2 (P)
SBN 7100 5122 0 (C)

This series of paper-back monographs is designed primarily to meet the needs of students of government, politics, or political science in Universities and other institutions providing courses leading to degrees. Each volume aims to provide a brief general introduction indicating the significance of its topic e.g. executives, parties. pressure groups, etc., and then a longer 'case study' relevant to the general topic. First year students will thus be introduced to the kind of detailed work on which all generalizations must be based, while more mature students will have an opportunity to become acquainted with recent original research in a variety of fields. This series will eventually provide a comprehensive coverage of most aspects of political science in a more interesting and fundamental manner than in the large volume which often fails to compensate by breadth what it inevitably lacks in depth.

Mr. McPherson's essay is a contribution to the theory rather than to the institutional section of this library; he is a philosopher rather than a political scientist. In discussing the meaning of the phrase 'grounds of political obligation', he is concerned only indirectly with the factual situation in any given political community and, as he says, only marginally with the history of political ideas. He seeks to understand the meaning of the concept itself. But his study is 'involved with real life', and especially with life in modern liberal democratic states. How is any theory of political obligation related to a given concept of society and of man's life in society? Can the whole concept be dispensed with? Not everyone will agree with Mr. McPherson's answer to this question but no one can fail to be stimulated by his arguments.

H.V W.

Contents

Acknowledgments

I am indebted to many people in the writing of this book:
to such writers of the past as David Hume and of the present as Professor John Plamenatz; to my students with
whom I have discussed these matters; to Professor J. L.
Evans, Professor H. Morris-Jones, Mr. Malcolm Murchison,
and Professor D. D. Raphael, for their ready agreement to
read parts of the book in draft; to Mr. J. F. Mackeson for
advice about the law; and to my wife who checked the
typescript and read the proofs. For the faults that remain,
none of these, but my own stupidity or obstinacy, must
be blamed.

T.McP.

1

Introduction

This book is about the concept of political obligation. By some this is regarded as not merely one among several concepts studied by political philosophers but as the central concept of their subject. By others it is looked on as relatively unimportant, or even as the source of serious confusion. Which of these opinions is right? As usual in philosophical matters there is much to be said on all sides. I try here to say at least something of what can be said. What I shall be concerned with chiefly is the so-called problem of the *grounds* of political obligation.

My interest is only incidentally in the history of views about political obligation, or in the history of theories about the grounds of political obligation. My concern is much more with the question what, if anything, could be meant at the present time by anyone who used the expression 'political obligation' or who offered as his own one of the standard theories about the grounds of political obligation that have come down to us from the past. A sense of history is a useful possession of the philosopher, but a study of what people in previous generations actually intended by certain expressions or theories does not of itself constitute a *philosophical* examination of those expressions or theories. The present book is intended as political philosophy.

I

What is political obligation? This is a question capable of being interpreted, and answered, in various ways. It can be seen as a kind of summing up of a set of factual questions, asking for information about such things as where power and authority reside in the State (or in a given State) and about people's beliefs concerning their leaders and about their attitudes towards those leaders. It can also, however, be seen as a question about the meaning of a concept. Not: what are *the facts about* political obligation? But rather: what is meant by the concept itself which is being used in stating those facts? My inquiry—though it ranges fairly widely—is basically conceptual and therefore philosophical in character.

My charge against certain writers is that they have been too general and abstract about the whole matter of the relations between subject and State. But, of course, to raise and consider the question whether a given approach is or is not too general and abstract is itself to be general and abstract—that is, methodological. If my discussion is itself general and abstract does this mean that it is 'merely' theoretical? This might seem to follow. Many would suppose so, anyway; and of them some would deplore the consequence, others welcome it. Some recent political philosophers have been rebuked for involving their subject more closely with real life than seems to their critics academically respectable. I do not agree with such critics. The activity of analysing concepts is undoubtedly different from that of solving practical difficulties: on the other hand, it is generally the existence of practical difficulties that makes it seem worth while to analyse concepts; and the analysis of concepts may well make easier the solving of such difficulties.

In one respect I do aim at the relatively particular. There is a limit to generalisation about 'the State'. States are of different kinds. Most of what I say in this book is intended to apply to modern liberal democracies—more particularly, to modern Britain. Some of what is said is, of course, capable of a much wider application.

In considering the notion of the 'obligation' of subject to State I have not felt it necessary to discuss the converse notion of what the State owes to the subject. There is nothing in this book about the 'limits' of political obligation. There is no systematic discussion of such concepts as authority, or sovereignty. It is not that I do not think all these matters important. It is not even that I do not think them in many ways relevant. But one must erect fences somewhere, and even if one were to shift them so as to enclose much more of this large field, a claim to having achieved any kind of completeness could still only be pretence.

2

Why obey governments?

The philosopher's interest in political obligation has been mainly in the problem of the *grounds* of political obligation—that is, in the question: Why ought we to obey the government? Some complexities present themselves when this question is examined closely.

Fact and value

It is necessary, to begin with, to consider the relation between 'Why *ought* we to obey the government?' and 'Why *do* we obey the government?'. There are important likenesses here, and important differences.

The most obvious difference is the following. When we ask why people *do* obey the government we expect an answer in terms of certain facts—facts about people's behaviour, about what they say, about what they believe, perhaps about their motives; facts about the penalties attracted by failure to obey; and so on. But when we ask why people *ought* to obey the government we do not expect an answer of this kind. Facts about what people do, or about what they say about what they do, or about why they do what they do, etc., are not altogether to the point (though not entirely off it either). It is a commonplace that you cannot answer a question about what people ought to do *simply* by pointing out what they do do, or speculating on what makes them do it. There are things that we have left undone which we ought to have done, and things that we have done which we ought not to have done: everyone recognises that there is a distinction here. What is not so clear is the nature of the relation between these notions; for that they are related is as undeniable as that they are different. This topic, under the title of the relation between 'is' and 'ought', or 'fact' and 'value', has been discussed by philosophers at length.

Alongside this difference there goes a likeness, or at any rate a connexion. There is no point in saying that people ought to do something that they are not able to do, and little point in saying that they are able to do something that people never actually do. We should not say that people ought to obey the government if we supposed this was something beyond their powers. It would be absurd to do so; and to point this out is merely to utter a truism. What is also important, however, is that we should hardly suppose that obedience to the government was something within men's powers unless we thought there was evidence that men actually did obey governments. We often do not know if something can be done until somebody tries to do it. The connexion between 'can be done' and 'is done' is not the same kind of connexion as that between 'ought to be done' and 'can be done'. A connexion, however, there undoubtedly is—empirical rather than logical. We should not say that people ought to obey governments unless we supposed that they can obey. 'Ought' implies 'can'. But that they can is (in general) evidenced by the fact that they do. If people habitually *dis*obeyed governments we should soon find ourselves asking whether they are *able* to obey (for any of a wide variety of reasons). Our answer to this question would decide whether we went on saying that they *ought* to.

Let us now turn to a second aspect of the relation between 'Why do we obey the government?' and 'Why ought we to obey the government?'. Both questions might be said to be asking for reasons, using the word 'reason' loosely. They differ, however, in that they are asking for reasons of different kinds.

We should probably reply to 'Why do we obey the government?' by making some remarks about either causes or motives. Causes and motives are two very different things; but it happens that, given the right circumstances, either may be mentioned in answers to this question. On the other hand, we should probably reply to 'Why ought we to obey the government?' by trying to give what we may call a justification. The distinctions here are not always sharp. The same answer—in the sense of the same set of words—might in some cases do for either question, though we should characterize it differently. For example, 'In the interests of the general happiness' would be a possible answer to either. If it were offered as an answer to the first, we should say that it stated our motive. If to the second, that it gave a justification.

'Justification' is perhaps not the ideal expression to use here. It does, however, serve the purpose better than certain others which tend to land one in obvious circularity. (Consider, for instance, the following. 'What are we asking for when we ask why we ought to obey the government?'— 'We are asking for something that will show that it is right, or, maybe, expedient'. But, depending on the force that we intend by 'ought' in the first place, the answers 'Because it is right', or 'Because it is expedient', do not so much give reasons as simply reiterate in other words that we ought. What we want is not to be told over again what we have begun by assuming, but rather to have our assumption justified.)

We pass to a third aspect of the relation between our

6

two questions. 'Why ought we to obey the government?' perhaps carries a certain suggestion of unwillingness. 'Why do we obey the government?' suggests rather merely a puzzlement. There are obvious practical implications here. The unwillingness—if, indeed, it does exist—might be dispelled or increased according to whether a satisfactory answer to the former question is thought to have been found. It might consequently seem to be in the interests of governments to persuade their subjects to adopt one or other of the standard theories of political obligation. Alternatively, they might be even better advised to encourage a transfer of their subjects' interest from the 'Why ought . . . ?' to the 'Why do . . . ?' question. In fact, however, governments (and subjects) on the whole show little interest in either.

But we must not make too much of the present difference. The 'Why do . . .?' question can also carry the suggestion of unwillingness. I may put the question 'Why do I do such-and-such?' as a first step in the process of getting myself to stop doing it. Equally, the 'Why ought . . . ?' question need not express unwillingness. In the context of philosophical discussion of political obligation —like the present discussion—it presumably does not. Each of these questions is in fact capable of being put with different kinds of emphasis. It depends how you interpret them whether you sense unwillingness or not. The philosopher's theoretical putting of such questions has a different 'feel' from that which would probably be present if the man in the street put them. There is a difference between the force of 'Why ought I to obey the government?' when this is put by someone who is wondering what, in general terms, are the grounds of political obligation and its force when put by someone who is wondering whether to make a false income tax return.

Commissives and contracts

So much for the relation between the questions 'Why ought we to obey the government?' and 'Why do we obey the government?'. I propose to turn next to a discussion of the relation between 'Why ought we to obey the government?' and certain other questions broadly of the same kind.

So far we have assumed that 'Why ought we to obey the government?' is the way to express the philosopher's problem about the grounds of political obligation. It is, indeed, *a* way. But we might also have expressed it by using such forms of words as 'Why ought *I* to obey the government?', or 'Why ought *people* to obey the government?'. And there are yet other ways of putting the problem that would have seemed, if I had started with them, equally good.

It will be convenient now to consider not these questions themselves but the statements that correspond to them: that is, 'We ought to obey the government', 'I ought to obey the government', 'People ought to obey the government'. Of these statements the second will occupy us chiefly.

There is an impersonality about the third as compared with the other two. To talk about what 'people' ought to do, as distinct from what 'I', or even 'we', ought to do, is to distance oneself. 'People' are generally other people. To discuss the problem of political obligation in terms of the obligations of 'people' (or, indeed, of 'citizens', or of 'the community') is to suggest an absence of personal involvement. It is to assume a theoretical attitude. Theoretical attitudes are appropriate to philosophers. However, what may appear only slight variations in the way a problem is formulated can result in alterations in the balance of theory and practice.

8

The notion of 'personal involvement' just referred to is a vague one. It is worth mentioning only because it leads on to something more precise than itself. Let us look rather closely at the form of words 'I ought to obey the government'.

There are various ways in which this might be understood:

1. I may utter this sentence as a kind of self-exhortation. Perhaps I have been backsliding and want to encourage in myself a more serious attitude to my duties as a citizen.

2. I may intend it as a statement about what I think or believe. I may be reporting a conviction that I happen to hold.

3. The utterance may record a solemn decision arrived at after a period of possibly long and tortured doubt.

4. Lastly, quite a different interpretation might be put upon what I am doing in uttering these words. This interpretation would, in my opinion, be a mistaken one. I do not even claim that anyone has ever made it. But what would be involved in making it, and the reasons why this interpretation is mistaken, raise issues of considerable importance. I might, in saying 'I ought to obey the government', intend neither to encourage myself, nor to report something about my beliefs, nor to record a decision, but to *commit* myself. That is, there might be present a certain performative element.

Performative utterances (the expression was introduced by J. L. Austin) are those in which the repeating of a formula, the saying of a certain set of words, itself, given the proper circumstances, constitutes the performance of an act. Thus, to say to someone (in appropriate circumstances) 'I promise' is to promise. To say these words is not to report that a certain act has taken place: it is itself to perform that act. Or, again, when the appointed person, the crowds being assembled for the purpose, breaks a bottle of champagne on the hull and says 'I name this ship *Queen Alexandra*', he has, *by saying those words*, performed the act of naming the ship.

Austin later developed a rather complex set of distinctions as a refinement on his original simple distinction between performative and constative utterances (constatives are *statements*—in the sense of utterances used to make a truth-claim only). In the later terminology, 'I ought to obey the government', on the present interpretation of it, would have to be classed as having the 'illocutionary force' of a *commissive*. Austin himself did not include 'ought' ('owe'?) in his list of verbs used typically in commissives. His list contains, among others, 'promise', 'undertake', 'contract', 'mean to', 'dedicate myself to', 'swear', and 'vow'. All these verbs, and others like them, are used when a speaker wants to commit himself to a certain course of action. A speaker intending to commit himself to obeying the government would be more likely to do it by saying 'I shall obey the government' than by saying 'I ought to obey the goverment'. (Austin does include 'shall' in his list of commissive words.) The interpretation we are now considering, however, invites us to regard 'I ought to obey the government' as having commissive force.

I have already remarked that this interpretation is mistaken.

To begin with, is there not something strange about the notion of the 'act' of committing oneself to obey the government—however exactly one may do it? Who ever performs this 'act'? Some people are professionally required to swear allegiance to the crown; but this is not the kind of thing that we are considering here. The most natural examples of performatives (promising, baptising, naming ships, etc.) are all of events that take place fairly often, and which usually follow conventional patterns long laid down and widely understood. But 'I ought to obey the government', interpreted as a performative, does not fit into this picture at all easily. There are no conventions about the saying of this; about whom one should say it to, about whether witnesses are needed, and so on. There are no conventions about using the sentence 'I ought to obey the government' as a performative because nobody so uses it.

There is an element of strain about the interpretation. 'I ought to obey the government', by contrast with 'I shall obey the government', has a preliminary air. It suggests not resolution but an attempt to bring oneself to the point of resolving. It is just possible that someone might seize upon the form of words 'I ought to obey the government' in order to commit himself to obeying the government; but it is much more likely that he would find some other way of doing it.

According to contract theory, we ought to obey the government because it is as if we had made a contract to do so. If someone were to say 'I contract to obey the government' (however unlikely it may be that anyone would say such a thing) there would be a strong case for regarding *this* as a performative utterance. I suggest that any plausibility there might seem to be in the interpretation of 'I ought to obey the government' as a performative utterance comes from the unconscious assimilation of 'I ought to obey the government' to some such form as 'I contract to obey the government' or 'I resolve to obey the government' or even 'I promise to obey the government'.

We need to be clear about what is involved here. Contract theory can only function as an answer to 'Why ought I to obey the government?' as long as being obliged to obey and being contracted to obey are understood to be different things: nothing is successfully explained that is explained merely in terms of itself. To *assimilate* 'I ought to obey'

11

to 'I contract to obey' clearly is to run the danger of offering an explanation that is no explanation. If to say 'I ought to obey . . .' is actually itself to be saying (in a less natural way) what is said by 'I contract to obey . . .', or 'I resolve to obey . . .', or 'I promise to obey . . .', then *'Because* I have contracted', or *'Because* I have resolved', or *'Because* I have promised' cannot give *the reason why* I ought to obey. The alternatives are clear. Either 'I ought to obey the government' is not interpretable as a performative utterance, or contract theory is not, as it has long been supposed to be, a theory of the grounds of political obligation. There is no doubt which of these conclusions would be the more surprising.

It may well be the case that contract theory gains some of what plausibility it has from the fact that it carries the suggestion of commitment. The commitment that can be present in the performative utterance 'I contract to obey the government' (essentially first person singular) is illegitimately carried over to 'People contract to obey the government' or 'We contract to obey the government' (where 'we' means something like 'all citizens').

This point may also be made in the following way. The notion of contract is historically linked with that of consent. The basic or standard situation of consent is where an individual consents. An individual, in giving consent to something, may, in appropriate cases (see Chapter 3), be said to be committing himself. He may also, in appropriate cases, be said to be entering into an obligation. Now we also make statements of the kind, 'The people, etc., consents'. To speak thus is to speak metaphorically. However, the basic or standard case of 'I consent' is, or so it seems to me, apt to get carried over illegitimately to the very different notions of 'The people consents' or 'The community consents', or even 'We consent'. If *I* consent, I may well commit myself, or I may involve myself in a

12

relation of obligation. But what sort of 'commitment', what sort of taking on of an 'obligation', do we have when 'the people' consents?

Theories about political obligation have themselves coloured our way of putting the problem of political obligation. This is not to be wondered at. It is on the whole the same people—philosophers—who have both formulated (indeed, perhaps, invented) and attempted to answer this problem. Every new generation is brought up on its predecessors' work. It is not surprising that the whole thing has come to run along almost too well-defined lines. Those who try to leave the rails find themselves bogged down in a vehicle unsuited for travel across open country. Contract theory, in particular, has had a long-lasting, and to some extent hidden, influence on the way in which the problem of political obligation has been conceived. The model of a contract itself suggests obligation; there is something binding about contracts. If we assume that the problem is one about a kind of *obligation*, then legal—and also moral—models come naturally to mind. The deep-seated influence of the contract model has furthered the belief that the problem is indeed one about a kind of *obligation*, and has helped to perpetuate formulations of the kind 'We *ought* to obey the government' and 'Why *ought* we to obey the government?'.

Orders and obedience

So far nothing has been said about the word 'government' in our original question 'Why ought we to obey the government?'. What precisely are we to understand by 'government'? Again, nothing has been said about the word 'obey'. Exactly what kind of obedience is meant here?

The expression 'obey the government' suggests a particular sort of model: that of the superior officer and his subordinate, or perhaps the Victorian father and his son. It is doubtful whether this model is an appropriate one for the relation between government and citizens. What one 'obeys' is, typically, *orders*. Not everyone is in a position legitimately to give us orders. Is 'the government' in this position? This is hard to say. What is meant by 'the government' here? In practice, certain individuals, agents of the government, might be acknowledged to be entitled in certain circumstances to give orders to 'us'; but not, I think, acknowledged by everybody or without dispute.

Let us suppose, for the sake of argument, that a policeman is an agent of the government—though 'government' here would presumably have to be taken in a sense other than that of central government. The law-abiding middle-class citizen might not agree that a policeman had the right to give him orders—give orders, that is, as opposed to make requests. He might, however, be willing to say that the policeman had the right to give orders to a criminal or suspected criminal. The police, the law-abiding citizen will all too likely be in the habit of saying, are the servants of the public and not their masters; but by 'the public' he means the law-abiding public—people like himself. The right of one man to give orders to another is normally dependent upon the acknowledgment of that right by the other.

The law-abiding citizen might be willing enough to say that we have an obligation to obey 'the government'. As long as 'the government' is impersonal, and 'obedience' understood in vague and general terms, he is content. But when the government takes the form of Constable Jones from the Police Station down the road, and obedience the form of action in accordance with *orders* given by Constable Jones to him, he hesitates.

Replace Constable Jones by the Prime Minister, and most of us would still, I think, resist any talk of *obedience* and *orders*. Replace the Prime Minister by the Queen, and the situation would still be the same. Bagehot wrote of the English people 'obeying' Queen Victoria; few would write in similar terms today. (This might not be true for a modern believer in divine right, if there are any such. And no doubt there are some people, apart from her employees, who, if confronted by the present Queen, would think it entirely proper that she should literally order them and that they should obey. The attitudes of people to their rulers differ widely.)

We may distinguish between what I shall call, perhaps tendentiously, proper and improper orders. We frequently use the word 'order' in situations where we should not want to say that the person 'ordering' has any authority to order. If someone says to me in peremptory tones, 'Put that down', I may well report afterwards that he ordered me to put the thing down and that I obeyed; for if he has a stick in his hand and a sufficiently fierce look in his eye I am unlikely to resist him. But 'proper' orders in general come only from recognised superiors to recognised subordinates within some particular sphere, like the Army or a business concern, and they are limited in their scope by the limitations (which will vary from one type of case to another) of the relationship. The office boy can, if necessary, be *ordered* by his employer to post the letters; he cannot (properly) be *ordered* by him to take the whole of his wages home to his mother.

I would not, of course, claim that orders from governments are in this sense improper orders. But the notion of the government 'ordering' us does go somewhat against the grain. It is a hangover from times of more personal rule. We can be required by government to do things, and legal penalties can be attached to our not doing them; but the language of 'orders' and 'obedience' used to describe this has, in my opinion, inappropriate associations. It is not the facts that I question—of governments requiring their subjects to do certain things and the subjects doing them—but the terminology of *orders* and *obedience* (and *obligation*) used to express those facts.

What has been achieved by this chapter? Principally, I hope, it has underlined the fact that the concept of political obligation is a far from simple one. Enough has been done to indicate the direction in which the argument will next proceed. The notion of political obligation must be broken down into its parts. 'We ought to obey the government' is a formula which covers a wide variety of more particular propositions.

The task to which I immediately turn is that of examining some of the standard theories about the grounds of political obligation.

3

Legal and moral models

There is a wide variety to be found among the theories offered as answers to the question, 'Why ought we to obey the government?' Those that I examine in this chapter and the next for various reasons seem the most worth examining, but I claim no completeness for my discussion.

The models that have commonly been used in the construction of answers are legal, moral, and (in a wide sense) paternal or patriarchal—usually singly, rarely in combination. On the whole, those who have offered an answer have offered one intended to be simple. The question itself is of great generality, and the answers have matched it in this. The more general the more simple: at least, until we start to probe deeper.

Contract and the legal model

Let us begin by looking at the kind of answer that is constructed to a legal model. This is the answer provided by contract theory—on one interpretation of that theory. Sometimes contract theory is interpreted rather informally, in terms of the notion of consent; and this has the effect of making us think of moral notions, like that of respect for persons. To be legitimate, government must be based upon consent, people say; and we think at once of the equality of man, of the right of the least among us to cast his vote and have it counted along with that of the greatest, and so on. At other times, however, contract theory is interpreted more formally, in terms of the notion of contract interpretation that we are first to consider.

itself, and the associations now tend to be of legal documents witnessed and sealed, and the like. It is this latter

An objection might be raised at the outset to the very notion of a legal model for political obligation. It might be said that it is impossible to interpret the social contract as a legal instrument since the point of contract theory is precisely to justify the existence of the whole legal apparatus. To attempt to explain political obligation as being itself a kind of legal contractual obligation would thus be to argue in a circle.

Does this objection hold? In general terms there certainly seems to be something odd about any procedure in which we are offered as an explanation of X something that itself needs to be explained in terms of X. However, words like 'explanation' and 'justification' can bear different meanings. We can attempt some kind of answer to the objection along the following lines. First, what we are concerned with here is the use of a legal *model* to explain political obligation. The suggestion is not that there is a literal, historical, explicit, legal contract to obey government. It is that the obligation to obey government may be illuminatingly interpreted to some extent after the fashion of a legal contract. Indeed, a main difficulty with contract theory is that it is clearly nowadays not to be taken literally. Secondly, consider the following analogy—which is, of course, only an analogy. In a painting the parts are dependent upon the whole, in the sense that they could not be parts of the whole unless there were a whole for them to be parts of; yet we may explain the painting by reference to one part of it which seems to us to contain the clue to the meaning of the whole. Unless political societies existed there could not be such a thing as a legal contract; but this of itself does not mean that we are altogether precluded from finding in the notion of a legal contract some clue to wider questions about the way in which political obligation is to be understood. Thirdly, although the notion of a legal contract may be dependent upon the existence of political society, it is not dependent upon the existence of any particular political society. Our obligation to obey *this* government may be interpreted without contradiction according to the model of a legal contract if we are so inclined, provided we already have the concept of political society and of the legal apparatus involved in political societies.

The objection, then, can be answered—up to a point. But in the course of answering it we have come up against the two most serious shortcomings of the contract theory. The first is its obviously non-literal character. To the question 'Why ought we to obey the government?' contract theory answers: 'Obey the government because it is as if you have entered into a contract to do so'. We will naturally retort: 'Yes, but have we really entered into such a contract?'. If we have not really entered into a contract but it is only as if we had, then our original question has been given an unsatisfactorily vague answer. If we are parties to a proper legal contract we are bound by it. If we are parties to a quasi-legal contract—or a quasi-legal quasi-contract—are we similarly bound? Unless the analogy can be adequately defended, contract theory, like any other theory of an as-if kind, says nothing. Otherwise, 'Obey the government because it is as if you had entered into a contract to obey' says no more than does 'Obey the government'. Reasons must be reasons, not hints or promises of reasons.

How much better it would be—we may say—if the contract theorist could throw off the obscuring cloak of simile and stand forth in legal (or even not too quasi-legal) respectability. 'We ought to obey the government because we *have* entered into a contract to do so.' If it were in fact the case that a given political society had originated in an express contract between subjects and rulers in which the parties explicitly accepted obligations of obeying and of ruling, then that fact would be relevant to the question why those people ought to obey that government. But no one supposes that we are today in such a situation. Whatever is being said when it is said that *our* obligation to obey the government is contractual, it is not that. And even if it were true as a matter of history that our State had originated in a contract of some kind between people and government in the past, this would not adequately answer the question why we today ought to obey the government.

The second chief shortcoming of contract theory resides in the fact that it is offered as a *general* theory about the grounds of political obligation. I have pointed out that, if someone insists on using it, it can be interpreted without contradiction as a theory about quasi-legal grounds of the obligation to obey a given government. It is not so clear that it is safe from criticism if interpreted as a theory about a supposed general obligation to obey government. Yet it is as such a general theory that it is commonly put forward. As a theory about the grounds of political obligation, the contract theory, it is supposed, needs to be expressed in a universal, timeless form, not attached to any particular historical circumstances. This is not to say that it must be totally detached from historical circumstances, but if it is to be rooted in historical circumstances they must be circumstances that recur for every new government or new generation of subjects. Indeed, the conditions for any theory about the grounds of political obligation, if it is to be a general theory, are that it must be derived from what are, or are alleged to be, universal features of human nature or universal human relationships, or basic moral principles supposed to be of universal validity, or historical circumstances of a kind that constantly recur in every generation. These are not easy conditions to meet. The alternative may well be to abandon the search for a *general* theory about political obligation.

Contract and legal obligation

But let us leave these difficulties and, on the assumption that there may yet be something to be learnt from the legal model, let us look more closely at the question how far the analogy with legal obligation holds. Consider the following view. When a political party solicits our votes in a general election it gives certain undertakings. If we vote for its candidates we are indicating a broad acceptance of its policies and are promising to give our allegiance to it in office if it is returned to power. The act of putting a cross on the ballot paper is the equivalent of signing a legal contract: the terms of the contract are contained in the party's manifesto, and in publishing its manifesto the party is indicating the acceptance for its own part of the conditions of the contract.

This is a pleasant picture, but in the conditions of modern Britain absurdly oversimplified. For one thing, it accounts much better for the relation between a government and those who actually voted for it than it does for that between a government and those who voted against it— who might, after all, be in a majority. Yet we are all presumably obliged to obey the government, whether we voted for it or against it, or did not vote at all. Is this obligation a contractual one in the case of about half the electorate and of another kind in the case of the other half? There is nothing wrong with this in itself, except that contract theory is supposed to be an attempt to explain in general terms why we *all* have an obligation to obey the government. The truth of the matter is that there is no single, simple answer to the question why we ought to obey the government. To the extent that all the standard theories are attempts to offer such a single, simple answer they are all equally at fault. It may be the case that some of us ought to obey the government for one reason, others for another. Or it may be that for all of us there is one reason why we ought to obey when the government asks us to do one thing, but a different reason when it asks us to do another.

It is sometimes objected to contract theory that we are born into the State and not contracted into it. This is certainly an objection to the applicability of the notion of contract as such. It is not, however, an objection to what I am at present supposing to be the basic aim of contract theory, the illumination of the notion of political obligation by the invocation of that of legal obligation. We find ourselves subject to all sorts of legal liabilities that we have not assumed by our own decision—the obligation to pay income tax, for instance. The kind of legal obligation exemplified by contracts is only one of several. If I am right in supposing that one aim of contract theory is somehow to explain political obligation in terms of legal obligation, then perhaps we ought to conclude that contract theorists have gone astray by choosing the wrong kind of legal obligation to model political obligation on. The obligation to obey the government is more like the motorist's legal duty of care to other road users in the law of torts—or, to take another example, it is more like the legal obligation to pay income tax (indeed, in part it *is* the obligation to pay income tax)—than it is like the obligation to honour a contract once entered into.

I do not want to press this point. There were other reasons why the specific legal model of contract should have been chosen. In particular, contract theory was intended to bring out the necessity for government to be based on the agreement, the 'consent', of the governed, rather than imposed on them from above; and this point would be missed if the specific model of a contract were replaced by some other kind of legal model. Nevertheless, if we take this wider interpretation, many of the minor objections to the theory cease to seem serious. The fact that governments do not actually appeal to the notion of contract when urging their policies on us, or the fact that subjects do not in general themselves think of their obligation to obey the government as one depending on contract—such objections, though they would tell strongly against the notion of contract itself (for if there is a contract the parties to it must know that there is a contract, even if they are unclear about its terms), do not dispose of the wider idea that political obligation may be interpreted as *some* kind of legal obligation.

However, even if the notion of legal obligation were taken in the widest possible sense there is still no good reason to suppose that it could, alone, throw an adequate illumination on political obligation. The legal model is only one of several. Parents may feel an obligation to do their best for their children when young, and children may feel an obligation to do their best for their parents when old. These obligations are not legal (or contractual) obligations. The father/child relationship has been invoked as well as the contractual relationship as a model to explain political obligation, and we shall be considering it in the next chapter. No doubt these two models have more to offer together than either has alone.

Consent

Let us turn to what I earlier called the informal interpreta-

C

tion of contract theory—that in terms of *consent*. On this interpretation the theory tells us that we ought to obey the government because (it is as if) we have consented to. But why should consenting to obey be supposed to constitute a ground for the obligation to obey?

We can distinguish a weak and a strong sense of consent. In the weak sense, I may consent to many things without really committing myself to them : here 'acquiesce' would be a possible synonym for 'consent'. In such cases the mere fact that I have consented to something is not a sufficient reason for my regarding myself as obliged. In so far as consent theories understand 'consent' in the weak sense (as does Locke) it is clear that they do not provide an adequate ground of political obligation. I suspect in fact that more often than not when we use 'consent' we use it in the weak sense. For what I am here calling strong consent we would probably use some other word or phrase, like 'commit oneself'.

We can also distinguish between cases where I consent to something that I ought not to have consented to and cases where my consent is to something morally good or morally neutral. Tempted by avarice, I may consent to join with someone in a scheme to defraud my employer. If in the end I fail to go through with it who will blame me on the ground that I have repudiated an obligation? Not even my partner in the proposed crime would be likely seriously to press a charge in language of this sort. It would be odd to say that I am *obliged* to carry out an immoral act, however strong my consent to it may have been.

It is clear, then, that the mere fact of having consented is not necessarily sufficient ground for being obliged—for either of the two reasons mentioned. What, however, of cases where I consent in the strong sense (as opposed to merely acquiescing) to something which is morally good or morally neutral (as opposed to morally bad)? Does consenting in *this* case constitute a ground of obligation? It seems to me that here, too—though for a very different reason—it does not. Whereas weak consent (mere acquiescence) and consent to a morally bad act might be said to be, in their different ways, not good enough to provide a ground for obligation, strong consent to a morally good or morally neutral act is, if anything, *too* good to provide such a ground. If I am not mistaken, in this kind of case to consent precisely is to take on an obligation. But the taking on of an obligation is not a ground of obligation. To have assumed an obligation is not a reason for, or a justification or ground of, being obliged. It is to be obliged. A reason for, or justification of, an obligation must be something other than the very assuming of the obligation itself.

What sort of thing then must it be? One possible reason or justification is to have entered into a legal contract—that is, to have formally contracted as opposed to having consented. If what we are looking for is reasons, justifications, or grounds, then the legal model is better than the moral. To invoke a (legal) contract would be to give some sort of reason for acknowledging something as an obligation. However much I may wish afterwards that I had never signed a contract, once I have signed it I am obliged to do what I have contracted to do. It is a perfectly proper answer to someone who points out to me that some course of action that I propose is really against my best interests to say, 'I know; but I've signed the contract; so I must go through with it'. It is true that contracts can be unilaterally broken, though usually sanctions will be attached to the breaking of them. But the point is that whether a man actually keeps his agreements or not, to say that he has legally contracted is always a proper reason or justification to give to someone who asks why a man is under an obligation. On the moral interpretation, however, to say that he has consented strongly is not, it seems to me, to give a reason why a man is under an obligation. And it does not give a reason why a man is obliged to do something because it is only another way of saying that he is obliged to do it.

What we call moral obligations seem to us to have some kind of primacy over other obligations—over what we call legal obligations, or political obligations. This primacy is one important factor in our calling certain obligations moral obligations in the first place. Now it is, it seems to me, because moral obligations have this primacy that we are reluctant to call upon them to, as it were, back up other obligations. To use them in this way, it seems, would be to demean them. Legal contracts, on the other hand, do not seem to most of us to have this special and untouchable character. The law is a device. Morality is not a device. Legal contracts can be put to use. Morality cannot be put to use. Devices are things that we can choose between, can use or can discard as we think best. To provide 'reasons' for an action suggests, rightly or wrongly, something of this sort. We may find good reasons one day only to find better ones the next. What seems a good reason to one may not to another. But moral obligations (and, of course, moral principles) we do not think exist for us to pick and choose between. Hence we do not think it appropriate to call upon moral obligations to provide 'reasons' for action.

Moral and prudential obligation

I have not so far mentioned a distinction that is commonly made in discussions of obligation and related matters—that between the moral and the prudential. Moral obligation and legal obligation are sometimes distinguished from each other on the ground that the law can appeal to sanctions and one's reasons for obeying the law may be fear of punishment, whereas this is not the case with morality. The question about political obligation would then be put in the form: Is the obligation to obey the government a moral or a prudential one?

It would be wrong not to refer to this distinction, but I do not make any explicit use of it in this book. To ask whether political obligation is moral or prudential is, in my opinion, to pose too simple and too committed a question.

4

King, custom and charisma

Explanations of the grounds of political obligation have not always been in terms of legal or moral models. Locke, in developing his political theory, was compelled to consider closely the kind of theory which sees the relation between ruler and ruled as that between parent and child. Contract theory has commonly been defined in contrast to the theory of divine right. To the extent that the monarch is seen as father of his people, and as entitled to their obedience as a father is entitled to the obedience of his children, the divine right theory may itself be said to be built up on moral notions; for there seems little doubt that the duty a child owes its parents is to be described as a moral duty. At the same time, the relation between parent and child also has properties peculiar to itself which requires its being taken as a separate heading. I shall interpret this relation in a wide sense in the present chapter, using it to draw together a number of views about the grounds of political obligation that are sometimes presented separately.

Paternalism

Paternalism in government is practised at the present time more than it is preached. In the past, however, from Plato onwards, it has had many persuasive advocates. But every wise parent knows that the obedience of his children may depend on getting from them some measure of agreement to his advice or instructions. Fathers often fall short of the ideal. There are bad fathers just as there are bad rulers, and more of them. Locke himself was writing of parental ideals rather than actualities. In his attempt to distinguish between political and parental power Locke had to contend with unenlightened views of both; and the effect of correcting the distortions of others' views was to soften somewhat the contrast he himself wished to point to. It would clearly be too simple to say, as one might be tempted to say but as Locke pointedly did not, that the difference is a straightforward one between power that is (properly) based on consent and power that is not. This would indeed be too simple; but there are other differences that can be suggested (we need not be concerned with the detail of Locke's own discussion of the matter).

There is the obvious difference that there is a biological relation between parents and their children that is absent as between rulers and ruled; but this is hardly worth mentioning, for no one today could seriously suppose that political power is literally the same thing as parental power, but only, at the most, that it is illuminatingly like it. Two other possible differences are the following. First, children grow up and pass from their parents' care. There is a temporal limit to the authority of parents over children and to the obligation of a child to obey (though not to honour) its parents : Locke himself makes this point. This is not the case with the relation between rulers and subjects. Secondly, rulers and ruled can change places; parents and children cannot.

Neither of these points of difference seems to me particularly significant. That children grow up and pass from their parents' care is no doubt generally the case in our society. But we all know of middle-aged bachelors who will hardly take a step except on the instructions of their mothers. Perhaps for some such people their condition is really better than would be one of greater 'freedom'. Superior age may not always mean superior experience and wisdom; but when it does there is no harm in acknowledging its authority. And once it is accepted that, even with quite young children, consent and (as far as it can be got) understanding, rather than unquestioning obedience, is the ideal in parent/child relations, the importance of a sharp break between the state of dependent childhood and that of independent adulthood is considerably lessened. Similarly, although it is true that rulers and ruled can change places and parents and children cannot, this does not seem to me to constitute a vitally important difference. A child cannot become his own parent, or a parent his own child. But a child can grow up to become himself a parent, and have the experience of being both parent and child; rather as a Member of Parliament is both ruler and ruled, for he is subject to the laws he helps to enact. And although in theory rulers and ruled can change places, in practice the Member of Parliament belongs to a dedicated and special group, and the ordinary voter has little real opportunity—let alone inclination—to join it.

Divine right

The paternalistic model assumes its least acceptable form in the theory of divine right. One motive behind divine right theory is the desire for absolute political authority, but this is on the whole just what people in the liberal democracies do not want. Even if they did want it they would probably look for it elsewhere: the word 'divine' is liable to strike them as foolishness or a stumbling-block. Yet the notion that men are not born equal is familiar enough. It ought to be; for it is true. So is the further notion that men are born dependent. And that there is something not quite right about the idea of a government as something 'set up' in a 'contract' by those who are subject to it is likely to meet with sympathy. It has been said of Filmer's presentation of the divine right theory that it is better on its negative than its positive side—that is, better as a criticism of contract theory. The presuppositions of contract theory are certainly open to criticism, and we may be very willing to abandon it—but less willing to abandon it when we see what is offered in its place. Even if the notion of contract or consent needs fuller consideration than some of its supporters gave it, to leap straight to that of the divine right of kings would be to leap backwards. Contract theory was at least moving in the right—'democratic'—direction. Paternalism need not take such extreme forms as those of absolutism or divine right. In theoretical political matters, as well as in practical, the art of not going to extremes is worth cultivating.

Charismatic authority

A form of paternalism more familiar in recent years is that of charismatic authority, to use Weber's term. Charismatic authority is personal authority, as contrasted with authority deriving from either a legal or a traditional basis. A stock example of this—on a relatively limited level—is that of the passenger who takes charge when a ship begins to sink and all about are panicking. Whoever can get power in such circumstances may be thought to have a right to it. We hear of men with 'magnetic personalities', of 'born leaders', and so on. At times, particularly times of crisis, people want to be led, and will respond to someone who has the confidence to put himself forward as their leader—Wesley, Hitler, Churchill. The felt need for a leader no

doubt plays a more important part in this than the possession of supposed superhuman powers by the leader himself,
but the leader does nevertheless have to be an exceptional
man. It is not easy to find examples of pure charismatic
authority, or, at any rate, long-lasting examples; for the
natural tendency is for the leader either to assume fairly
soon some existing office (Chancellor, Prime Minister,
etc.), or to create an office for himself or at least submit
to its being created for him by his followers; and then with
the passage of time it becomes difficult to distinguish between the authority that the leader possesses in himself and
which cannot be transferred and that which belongs to the
office and which can.

In other words, as Weber himself insisted, pure charismatic authority is very seldom found, except for short
periods and in relatively localised situations. In the political situation of a modern liberal democracy it cannot be
more than an element in leadership, never the whole. This,
it seems to me, constitutes a strength rather than a weak-
ness of the notion of charismatic authority. Some of the
criticism levelled against this notion seems to depend on
the belief that if it is to be taken seriously it must be kept
pure, and that any weakening of its purity is an objection
to it. This is only one manifestation of the general assumption that the standard theories of political obligation are
mutually exclusive, and that each can only be defended
at the expense of the others. But in this matter strength is
more likely to lie in combination than in isolation.

Every leader needs a policy—even if it be expressed in
only very general terms. In the case of the man who takes
charge on the sinking ship the policy is clear—survival.
The others do not follow him altogether blindly. They
follow him because they believe he can help them to
achieve the end they all want. However strong his personality, if he commanded them to cast themselves into the sea

and destroy themselves they would be unlikely to follow. Hitler in the Germany of 1933 and Churchill in the Britain of 1940 were able to inspire men to follow them, but they were obeyed not blindly but because they gave promise of achieving the future that their followers wanted. As Weber himself pointed out, charismatic authority is unstable. Almost everything depends on the success or failure of the leader in achieving what his people look to him to achieve. If he fails he may be dispensed with. But a charismatic leader, because he has superior powers of leadership, is likely to succeed in carrying the people with him, and therefore likely to get his policy put into effect. It is better to obey a charismatic leader with the right policy than a non-charismatic leader with the right policy: better because he is the more effective leader. But it is not the charismatic quality of his leadership alone which gives him the right to demand our obedience. It is his effectiveness in putting a certain policy into effect. In the end it is the policy which counts. To make his charismatic qualities themselves the sole ground of our obedience would be like saying that a certain leader ought to be obeyed because he is good at getting people to obey him.

Because the charismatic powers of a leader are not in themselves adequate ground of political obligation is not a good reason for denying charismatic authority any place whatever in a theory of political obligation. The tendency to go for all or nothing is to be resisted. In practice, the charismatic qualities of leaders do play some part in the political systems even of liberal democracies. The 'image' of a leader that is built up through press and television, however synthetic it may be, can still have considerable charismatic overtones. And some of the right that a man has to be obeyed may well come from his own qualities as a man and not merely from his office.

Traditionalism

The divine right theory and the theory of charismatic authority, in their use of the model of parenthood, interpret that model directly in personal terms. The king is a kind of father, and so is the charismatic leader. This is only to be expected: after all, parents are persons. But a less direct interpretation is also possible, one in which parenthood is depersonalised into an abstraction. Alongside the God-appointed monarch and the self-appointed genius there stand custom and tradition, order and stability (it is of the essence of the matter that the distinction between these pairs of ideas is not examined as closely as it ought to be). The emotions engendered by tradition or custom can sometimes be very much those engendered by the monarch believed to rule by divine right, or by the charismatic leader. Experience and wisdom are by some supposed to reside in 'tradition'; as they are supposed, particularly by parents, to reside in parents. Tradition is abstractified parenthood.

Behind the theory of traditionalism lies the belief that the *status quo* never needs to be justified in the way proposed changes do. This is a 'safe' attitude. Nothing venture, nothing win—but nothing lose either. In the field of morals it is the attitude of Aristotle, or in more recent times of G. E. Moore: the moral principles that we have inherited from our forefathers should not be lightly questioned; it is always preferable to adopt the principles of one's society rather than to be forever striving to 'work out one's own position'. There is no particular virtue in having a moral position of one's own. The moral position of other people is quite good enough—when it represents the combined wisdom of generations. This kind of conservatism or conventionalism about morals has come under strong attack from time to time. It is seen as representing a kind of moral

34

infantilism, or at best moral adolescence. Moral adulthood, the critics maintain, requires in a man that he hold the moral principles that he does hold as the result of reflection and conscious decision on his own part. They may, of course, be identical with those of his teachers, but the reason why he holds them must not be simply because he has been taught them but because he has consciously decided to make them his own. There is something to be said for both sides in this dispute, but I shall not pursue the matter here.

There are three important shortcomings in the traditionalist view :

1. To begin with, the traditionalist (as I have already hinted) too readily identifies order and stability with that which is customary. It is true that absence of change, adherence to customary social relationships and customary ways of doing things, is the commonest way of achieving —or rather of not losing—order and stability. But this needs closer examination. In one sense of the phrase 'order and stability' it is probably analytic to say that absence of change, or adherence to custom and tradition, means order and stability; for we may quite literally *mean* by 'order and stability' precisely 'absence of change'. To say that a society is 'stable' is another way of saying that it is 'not changing'. However, this is to use the phrase 'order and stability' in a trivial sense. The expression can also be used more informatively. It is a *good thing*, most people would hold, for a society to be ordered and stable. Order and stability are contrasted with civil *dis*order, where this implies danger to life or property. Now in this sense, the notion of the customary, that which is traditional, is by no means identical with the notion of order and stability. There might be a society in which civil unrest, insurrection, banditry, etc., were customary or traditional. In such a society, there might be those who longed for order and

35

stability, and who saw no way of getting them other than by a break with custom and tradition.

A certain confusion between these two senses of 'order and stability' tends to be involved in traditionalism. Order and stability in the State is a good thing: on this practically everyone will agree. But there are several ways of achieving order and stability, and adherence to custom and tradition is only one of them. Adherence to custom and tradition seems to have a privileged position among the various methods of achieving order and stability because of the connexions in meaning between certain uses of the expressions 'tradition', 'absence of change', and 'stability'. To make the point in other words, the traditionalist is in danger of proving too much. In so far as his case rests, covertly, on an identity of meaning, in some uses, between 'adherence to tradition' (='absence of change') and 'stability' (='absence of change'), his position reduces to a truism.

Whether a child is disposed to conform or to rebel, what he must conform to or rebel from is presented to him in the guise of the attitudes, opinions, customs, of his parents —or of parent-surrogates like clergymen or teachers. As far as the family is concerned, conformity tends to mean order and stability, rebellion tends to mean disorder and instability. To the political traditionalist, the State is like one big family. In the place of Father, who in the family represents custom and tradition, there stand Custom and Tradition themselves. We may conform or we may rebel. But we know from our experience of family life that conformity is more likely to lead to peace, and if we rebel we go into it with our eyes open.

What really matters is the order and stability that may be achieved by adherence to tradition; not adherence to tradition in itself. But the traditionalist is the man who sees, or thinks he sees, that conformity to tradition is more likely than is breaking with tradition to lead to order and stability. He is probably right in this. On the other hand, order and stability alone are not enough, and men have sometimes judged it necessary to upset tradition in the interests of, say, freedom, or what they believe to be freedom. The traditionalist is forever hovering on the brink of mistaking the empirical connexion between adherence to tradition on the one hand and order and stability on the other for a necessary one. It is this that helps to give him the authority to resist proposals of change.

2. There is a tendency in traditionalism to link too closely fact and value—how things are with how they ought to be. This distinction has already been touched on in Chapter 2. Because things are such-and-such is not a sufficient reason why they ought to continue so. I do not say it is no reason at all. But it is not in itself a sufficient reason. I am not suggesting that traditionalism involves any kind of crude and obvious confusion of fact and value. Perhaps some versions of it do, but I am not concerned to argue this. Clearly, no sophisticated traditionalist would commit so simple a mistake. But the traditionalist, though he may not confuse value with fact, does tend to see value too much as determined by fact—and, at that, passing fact, fact limited to particular States or societies. Part of the meaning of value, of the 'ought-to-be', is a reaching for the ideal, a refusal to be limited by things as they are now and have been.

Of course, the reader may say, the traditionalist is not inclined to 'reach for an ideal', at any rate where the 'ideal' is something as yet not realised, something in the future. It would be absurd to expect him to. To be a traditionalist *means* to have one's eyes fixed on the past and on realities, rather than on the future and on idealities. Or rather, for him, the past—and the present—may *constitute* the ideal. To expect him to be otherwise is to expect the traditionalist not to be a traditionalist. But the point is not a trivial one.

However close the link in a given case between what is and what ought to be, these notions themselves are still separate in meaning. Too close an identification of each with the other does not make for clarity. The ideal may lie in the past or it may lie in the future. More probably, it lies in a mixture of the two. More probably still, there is no such thing anyway as *the* ideal. What is true, however, is that some have seen politics in terms of ideals (political ideals, not moral ideals); and this seems to involve a looking to the future as well as to the past. Consider the force of the independence of India as an ideal. No doubt it is often no more than human inertia that leads men to adhere to tradition and custom. Sometimes it is more than that; and, indeed, the mechanisms here are varied and complex. I am not, however, concerned with this question from psychological, sociological, or anthropological points of view. My interest is in the question : How far does the appeal to tradition constitute an adequate theory of the grounds of political obligation? It seems to me that it does have some contribution to make to such a theory, if we want to construct one. But the appeal to tradition needs to be combined with an appeal to underlying reasons. By all means retain the social relationships that we have inherited. But not simply because this is how things have been done before, and not simply because these are the traditional social relationships. At the very least, we need to behave thus because we believe—if we do believe it—that this is the best way to maintain order and stability in society. Better still, we need to hold some view about why we think that order and stability are valuable—namely, as tending to some further end.

3. The customs and traditions of a society do, despite the efforts of the traditionalist, manage to change from time to time. Over a long period they may change, by easy stages, so radically as in the end to be totally different from what

they were in the remoter past. Which traditions and customs are we to follow? In general, the traditionalist would answer : those of the present and the immediate past. Some, however, might insist on going back beyond these, to customs more remote, and totally opposed to those of the immediate past, which they believe to be the 'real' tradition of their society. There lies in this the possibility of self-contradiction in the appeal to tradition.

Good and bad paternalism

One final comment on the whole paternalistic approach. The father/child relationship is one which alters to some extent from century to century, and also one which in any given instance develops as both father and child—especially child—grow older. Locke, for one, clearly recognised the importance of the latter of these changes. Even so, he did not, I think, give it as much weight as he might have done. If one is to be a paternalist in politics (which Locke, of course, did not consider himself to be) it makes a difference whether the precise father/child relation which is taken for the model is that between a father and a small child or that between a father and an adolescent. This did not matter so much in previous ages, but it does matter today. It has been one of the less fortunate features of colonialism that it has not sufficienty recognised this difference, as it is often a mark of ordinary parenthood that it does not recognise it.

Perhaps it is not so much that paternalism itself is at fault as that paternalists have tended to go for the wrong part of the model. It is only unimaginative parents who are surprised when the treatment they think appropriate for their children when small does not work when those children are older. Victorian parents and Victorian paternalists alike are out of place. The wise parent is not surprised or

39

hurt at the wish of his adolescent children to rule their own lives. I am far from wishing to recommend paternalism as a proper attitude in either home or colonial affairs. But it is perhaps capable of being formulated by a determined present-day paternalist in a version less inadequate than the usual ones. 'They are just children' may be insulting, but it is also worth making more precise even if ultimately it is rejected. There are children and children. In particular, there are small children and there are children so much larger as almost to have passed beyond being children. Treating grown-up people as adolescents is better than treating them as toddlers. Of course. to treat them as grown-up people would be better still.

5

Cutting down to size

Why have some political philosophers felt it necessary to hold theories of political obligation? It is significant that not all philosophers have felt this need. Greek speculation, for instance, did not lead in this direction.

Individualism versus collectivism

Those who have made use of the concept of political obligation have on the whole tended to be individualists. Locke is the obvious example.

Political philosophers have contributed greatly to our understanding of man and of man's life in society and in the State. But they have not contributed in the way that social scientists have contributed. Their method is not to make generalisations on the basis of the evidence of how man as a political animal behaves—nor to offer theories which can be tested by further evidence of the same kind. The political philosopher tends to inhabit a region of abstractions and ideals. This is not to say that there are not people who are both political philosophers and political 'scientists' (Aristotle set the example in this): but I am writing of their strictly philosophical activities. The theories of political philosophers may be criticised on the ground of internal inconsistency. But it is often difficult to criticise them on external grounds. There are, naturally, two sides to this coin. If it is often difficult to find what looks like a good reason, apart from logical inconsistency, for rejecting the views of a political philosopher, it is equally difficult to find a good reason for accepting his views: logical *consistency* alone will not guarantee a theory.

It is political philosophies of an individualistic kind that have needed the concept of political obligation. But why accept an individualistic philosophy, like that of Locke, as opposed to a collectivistic one? Reasons one in fact finds offered for preferring one political philosophy to another frequently tend to be of a temperamental kind. (We are easily reduced to respecting Hobbes for his style and his powers of argument while deploring his absolutism; or to admiring Locke for having helped to influence the eventual development of democracy while regretting his inconsistencies; or acknowledging Rousseau's visionary insights into the importance of community while wishing the 'totalitarian' elements of his work did not exist. And so on. All this is not very satisfactory. Much discussion of the work of political philosophers does, however, proceed in this kind of way.) Suppose there is no logically compelling reason for accepting an individualistic political philosophy. Then the companions of individualism, such as the concept of political obligation, become, at the very least, more avoidable.

This is to put the matter at its lowest. It may turn out after all that there is in fact good reason for *rejecting* individualism (at least, as far as its involvement with the concept of political obligation is concerned); this we have not yet considered. At present I wish to make only the relatively mild point that individualism and collectivism represent two persisting and fundamentally different attitudes to political questions neither of which, generally speaking, offers any very strong arguments in its own support. Fundamental attitudes, indeed, are not easily argued for. In so far as political obligation is associated with one of these fundamentally opposed attitudes and not with the other, its importance for political philosophy *as a whole* may be said to be lessened.

Why does individualism need the concept of political obligation, whereas collectivism seems to be able to do without it? One reason is obvious enough. To someone who sees men as individuals, and begins from notions of individual rights, government is apt to appear as Them, set over against Us. To someone who sees individuals as essentially parts of a larger whole, the community, government may well appear as Us, rather than Them. I remarked in the first chapter that words like 'ought' and 'obligation' often carry a certain suggestion of reluctance. The notion that governments *ought* to be obeyed, and even more the question '*Why* ought we to obey the government?', are not unlikely to occur to someone who regards his individual rights as paramount and government as consisting of people other than himself. To the collectivist, to whom the rights of the individual are of much less importance than the interest of the community and who tends to see government as that community in a certain aspect of itself, the notion that governments *ought* to be obeyed, with its implication of reluctance, is apt to seem unreal, and naturally therefore so does the rather grudging question '*Why* ought we to obey the government?'.

An individualist, who may suppose that because he himself has a theory of political obligation so ought everyone else to have one, may be tempted to construct such a theory on behalf of the collectivist. There are obvious advantages in attempts to force all political philosophies into the same mould. It makes things easier for everybody if we can persuade ourselves that the disparateness of thinkers lies in their attempting different answers to the same questions, rather than, more tiresomely, different answers to different questions. On a more respectable level, someone might argue that the question 'Why ought we to obey the government?' is at any time an important one. If a philosopher has failed to ask it directly, then others must ask it for him and answer it as best they can on the basis of the things that he does say. The individualist might argue, in other words, that a political philosophy is in an important way incomplete unless it contains, or can be made to contain, a theory about political obligation. If one is convinced that political obligation is an important concept for political philosophy one will be strongly inclined to so read the theories of opposing political theorists as to find this concept somewhere in them; either that, or perhaps cease to take them seriously as political theorists. But this is much harder to do than it may look. The whole spirit of collectivism is resistant to such attempts.

Society: artificial or natural?

We have noted that the supporters of political obligation tend to be individualists. We may now go on to note that some of them tend also to be people who regard society as artificial rather than natural. These points are, of course, closely related. Here I have contract theorists chiefly in mind.

Contract theory may seem to be the paradigm of political theories which require for their adequate statement the concept of political obligation. But contract theory takes several forms, as we have noted, and not all versions of it involve the notion of the artificiality of society—of government, no doubt, but not of society. I do not wish to give any false impressions here. I do not wish to say that everyone who has put forward views about political obligation believes that society is an artificial creation. Nevertheless, the fact that some clearly do is sufficient reason for examining the matter more closely.

Those who wish to stress the *naturalness* of States, or of societies, or of the relation between rulers and subjects, have generally turned to the model of the family. Surely nothing in the field of human relationships could be less 'artificial', more 'natural', than the very basic relationships that obtain in the family?

Yet what precisely is meant by 'natural' here? To say that the family is a natural unit might mean that it is not set up by the free decision of its members, but exists somehow already and independent of their decisions. But this is false. A family comes into existence initially through the free decision of two individuals to marry. And, while it is true that the children of that marriage do not make their entrance into the family as a result of their own free decisions, they may certainly subsequently by free decision repudiate their membership. The unit formed by a childless couple is as entitled to be called a family as is any other; and far from its being the case that such a family is not set up by the free decisions of its members the reverse is true. Or consider the extension of such families by the adoption of children : here there may well be some element of decision on the part of the adopted children as well as on that of the adoptive parents. Indeed, there are probably in the family enough elements of contract and free decision by independent persons to make it a usable model for the contract theorist as well as for the paternalist. The view of the State as a kind of super-family is capable of interpretation in contrary senses.

Is there then some other way of understanding the statement that the family is 'natural', some way other than that it is not set up 'artificially' by the free decisions of individuals? There are several other ways. In particular, the statement may mean that the family is the 'natural' psychological unit, in that apart from family life people are somehow less integrated, less happy, etc. Here 'natural' is opposed not to 'artificial' so much as to, say, 'dispensable', and carries the suggestion of that which is 'proper to' or 'necessary for' human beings. Though one could conceive of different kinds of basic human relationship systems, nothing else answers the needs of human beings as family life does. This may well be true.

The ambiguities of 'natural' do not make it easy to see what is meant by the view that the family is the natural human unit. But one thing seems clear. Society and the family (or the State and the family) are different things, and will always remain different things, however many points of likeness between them one cares to develop. That one of the pair is called natural can never completely determine that the other is to be called natural. Plato thought that society is natural to man (that is, essential for man) but that the family is a bad influence on the guardian class and for them should be done away with. He did not make man's sociability depend on the 'naturalness' of the family.

Neither the charismatic nor the traditionalist theory could plausibly be said to require the belief that society is artificial. The whole question is irrelevant to the former, and the latter probably is slightly more favourably inclined to the reverse belief. But the divine right theory, in so far as it leans on the model of the family, is, as I hope I have shown in the foregoing analysis of the 'naturalness' of the family, by no means so committed to the view that society is natural as is often supposed. The use of the family model has been widespread and varied throughout the history of political theory, and its users have not always been divine right theorists. The model has, it is true, generally been associated with the notion of the 'naturalness' of society, but this is an association that should not be accepted too uncritically.

To sum up the preceding part of the discussion. Some of those who accord centrality to the concept of political obligation tend to hold theories which treat society as artificial rather than natural—namely, some contract theorists and even, it may be, divine right theorists to the extent that they make use of the model of the family. We see once again, as we saw in the case of individualism *versus* collectivism, that the concept of political obligation tends to accompany particular kinds of outlook in political theory. It has not been found necessary for all kinds of theory.

Duty versus love

Political obligation is likely to connect in the moral sphere with an ethics of duty rather than an ethics of love. To someone whose life is organised in terms of love, loyalty, friendship, questions about what he *ought* to do, as opposed to what he freely and 'naturally' does, are apt to seem unimportant. It has been held by some that feeling loyalty towards one's community, or even absorption into it, of the kind that Rousseau wanted, is likely to exclude an interest in political *obligation*. This may well be so, although loyalty, like most virtues, is something that people can be conscientious about and can feel obliged to cultivate. There is certainly in general a different atmosphere about an ethics which lays its stress on duty from that of one which lays its stress on love. I have perhaps made too many generalizations already, but it does seem that believers in political obligation are more interested in duty than in love, loyalty, or patriotism.

Two objections

What I have tried to do in this chapter is to discuss three

respects in which theorists whose work gives prominence to political obligation seem to differ from those whose work does not. They tend to be individualists rather than collectivists, they include as an important sub-group people who regard society as artificial rather than natural, and they probably tend to hold an ethics of duty rather than love. That is, they take up one or more of a limited number of attitudes, to each of which there are clear alternatives. If we reject any of the three positions that have been discussed, the attractions of a theory of political obligation are that much diminished. And all of these positions can be questioned.

Two possible objections to my line of argument in this chapter suggest themselves:

1. Someone might object as follows: 'The expression "political obligation" is one that has on the whole been used by people writing *about* the views of classical political theorists rather than by those theorists themselves. It is customary to say of certain theorists that they hold such-and-such theories of political obligation even although the expression "political obligation" itself is not used by them. Does this not make comparisons between writers who "have felt the need of" a theory of political obligation and writers who have not difficult to substantiate?

My answer to this objection is that whether the expression 'political obligation' be used or not, or whether the question 'Why ought we to obey the State?' be put in that precise form or not, the *concept* of political obligation is clearly implied in the writings of some theorists as it is not in those of others.

2. In the second place (to make again a point touched on in an earlier section of this chapter), someone might object as follows: 'The appeal of the concept of political obligation may well be to a relatively limited group of

political philosophers, but that does not mean that the concept is not nevertheless needed by any political theory,
whether its proponents realize it or not'.

This is easily answered. In the field of political theory
the test for what needs to be explained is what people want
to have explained. If many philosophers have not felt that
they need the concept of political obligation this is a sufficient reason for saying that a theory of political obligation
is not an essential part of all political theories. We shall later
see that there are other reasons, but there is at least this one.

The argument of this chapter is aimed at diminishing the
importance of theories of political obligation. However,
nothing in it is supposed to constitute a *refutation* of any
such theory. The chapter is aimed merely at putting the
theories, and the concept of political obligation itself,
in proper perspective. At the same time, putting things in
perspective, or cutting them down to size, can sometimes
be as effective a weapon against them as a more formal
undermining of the kind to which we now proceed.

6

The general and the specific

Can there be a simple answer to the question, 'Why ought we to obey the government?' It is unlikely that there can be a simple answer to a question that is not itself simple. Some of the complexities of this question have already been noted, and there are others. In the present chapter I argue (on the basis of this complexity) against the view that it is possible to devise a simple general theory of political obligation.

The generality of the question

No single theory of the standard kind offers an answer that is plausible in all cases. Attempts to argue that, for instance, political obligation is really moral obligation, are neither here nor there. The truth of the matter is that sometimes it is and sometimes it is not. If loyalty is a moral virtue, how far is the obligation to fight for one's country in time of war a moral obligation? What is the relation between loyalty and patriotism? Such questions are impossible to answer in general terms. It depends on circumstances. Moral considerations may well come into such a case, though not necessarily; and to what extent depends on many things.

It does not take much thought to realise that none of the theories that have been put forward will serve as sole and complete answers to all specific questions about the grounds of political obligation. There is in reality not a single question to which they equally serve as answers. There are many questions. The reason why this is so has already been mentioned. The general notion of obedience to government, because it involves action, must be broken down into specific actions or kinds of action if it is to be seen to have any content. To tell someone that he ought to obey the government is to tell him very little. He will rightly ask: But just what must I *do*? There are many answers to this. He must pay his income tax, he must halt his car at a red traffic light, he must take up arms if required in time of war; and so on, through a list of many hundreds or thousands of items.

When obligation to obey the government is broken down in this way—as it must be broken down—we see the inadequacy of a single general theory of political obligation. 'Obligation to obey the government' is in reality only a useful shorthand. We cannot be forever producing a long list of the kinds of things that are subsumed under it. There is a place for the general phrase. It may not occur much in the thinking of the ordinary citizen, but writers on politics have found it useful. However, failure to see it for what it is can give rise to too ready an acceptance of general theories. It is true that general questions call for general answers. There would be no harm in this so long as the general answers were capable of being broken down in a way precisely parallel to that in which the general question must be broken down. Then each specific question would have its specific answer within the terms of a single theory. If things actually worked out in this way one would have fewer quarrels with general theories of political obligation. Unfortunately, they do not. No one general theory breaks down so as to cover all cases equally easily: theory *A* will work well enough for cases *a, b, c,* but not cases *d* or *e*; theory *B* for cases *c, d, e,* but not cases *a* or *b*.

The general question is the same for all the theorists: 'Why ought we to obey the government?' But the answers are presented as rivals. They are designed not to supplement each other but to exclude each other. And wherever there are a number of theories in competition with each other it is a fair supposition that none of them covers all the facts equally well. The success of one (it is hoped by its proponents) must mean the failure of the others. There has never been universal agreement on any single general theory of political obligation. The failure of any of them permanently to oust all the others may be put down, firstly, to the tendency to pose a question in general terms without considering sufficiently closely the need to cash it in terms of the more specific questions which it sums up, and, secondly, no doubt, to a tendency (to the extent that the need to cash the general question may be accepted) to cash it in terms of those specific questions that are most susceptible of an answer in terms of the favourite theory. It is never surprising that a theory seems plausible to its supporters.

If we were to insist on having a general theory of political obligation it would have to be (against the protests of the theorists of the past) an eclectic one. Although no single theory provides the whole answer, each of them might perhaps provide some part of the answer. It may be that we ought to obey the government in part because we have made a kind of contract, in part because we have a moral obligation, in part because it is customary to obey the government, in part because some political leaders have powers of personality by which we are right to be impressed. Such an eclectic general theory could certainly be constructed. But it would have little practical use. The important questions about political obligation are the specific ones. Men who are not political theorists are not likely to ask themselves, 'Why ought we to obey the government?' They are more likely to ask, 'Why ought I to pay this demand for income tax?' or 'Why ought I to accept this call to military service?' To such questions the eclectic general theory provides an answer of a kind, but an answer that needs interpretation. Some element or elements of the eclectic answer will need to be drawn out and emphasised —different elements in different cases. We are not much better off with our eclectic theory than we should be with a group of separate, competing theories. Choosing one element out of a single complex answer is not very different from choosing one answer from among a number of separate ones.

Is there then no one theory of political obligation that stands out above all others? Or is there no element of the single eclectic theory that counts for more than the rest? Many would be inclined to say that there is. And the majority of them would probably maintain that if there is such a central theory, or central core to an eclectic theory, it is connected somehow with morality. This is not surprising, in view of the use of the word 'obligation'. As long as this word is used, the flavour, faint or strong, of morality is likely to remain with what is called 'political obligation'. Part of what needs to be done if this concept is to be made clearer is to try the effect of calling what philosophers have called political *obligation* by some other name. It is clear that as long as we put the question to ourselves in the form 'Why *ought* we to obey the government?' the notion of morality is likely to have an advantage—possibly an unfair advantage—over other notions. I do not myself believe that there is any one theory of political obligation, or any one element of an eclectic theory, that deserves preeminence over all the others; and in particular I do not believe that a moral theory or element enjoys any such privileged position.

What, who, and how

Let us now turn to look more closely at some of the variety that we find when we attempt to break down into its component parts the complex notion of obedience to government. Why ought we to obey the government? That depends on these three things at least: what the government is asking us to do; what is meant by 'the government'; and how the appeal is made.

1. There are a great many things covered by the phrase 'what the government asks us to do'. To repeat the examples I have used already: stopping at red traffic lights, paying income tax, performing military service. Why do I accept the obligation to stop at red traffic lights? An honest answer would probably be in terms of self-preservation. Need we look further? Under which theory of political obligation does stopping at red traffic lights most naturally fall? If under any, then under a theory like that of Hobbes, which, on the commonest interpretation, is a theory of expediency or self-preservation, though he is also a contract theorist. But it would be straining things to insist on explaining a perfectly ordinary instance of stopping at red traffic lights under the notion of contract, or for that matter of any kind of paternalism. I do not say that it could not be done; but the machinery seems unnecessarily cumbersome for the task. Why ought we to pay income tax? There may be many things at work here. It may depend on what we think the taxes are going to be spent on. If we believe strongly in the principles of the Welfare State but disapprove of the amount of money spent on armaments we may feel an obligation to pay part of our taxes and a counter obligation to withhold another part. The acceptance of the

54

obligation to respond to a call to military service may be explained in terms of such moral, or apparently moral, notions as loyalty, in terms of patriotism (which may or may not be a moral notion), in terms of the charismatic qualities of a leader, in terms (once again) of self-preservation, and so on.

It might be said that my traffic lights example is too trivial, that this is not the sort of thing that the framers of theories of political obligation were trying to account for. This, however, cannot be said of the income tax and military service examples. But, in any case, any theory that purports to explain in general terms why we ought to obey the government surely must, if it is to be adequate, apply to cases like all of these. Is there a single answer to the question 'Why ought we to obey the government?' that makes equally good sense as applied to all three examples, without grossly over-simplifying the varied issues involved in them?

2. Let us pass to the second point mentioned above: what is meant by 'the government'? Just as the government can be regarded as the agent of the people as a whole, so governments themselves need to work through agents. Obedience to government may mean 'obedience' of some impersonal directive issued by unseen and unknown civil servants in Whitehall, or it may be a much more face to face affair, involving someone who in his private capacity is a friend. It is clear to begin with that the *reasons why* we obey may well vary as between such cases. The reasons why we refrain from parking by a sign reading 'Police Notice: No Parking' or the equivalent, may depend on whether we are at home or abroad; or on whether disobedience would make extra work for the kindly constable who lives down the road and whose wife is always so good about it when our children throw their ball into his garden; or 'merely' for an impersonal organisation called 'the

55

police'. But it is not just the reasons why we do in fact obey that would vary. So might. in consequence, the grounds of the felt obligation to obey. We might consider—perfectly properly, in my opinion—that the reasons why we *ought* to obey are different in different cases. When the constable is someone whom we know and like this may well provide an additional reason why we *ought* not to park by the local 'No Parking' sign. Perhaps this additional reason is a 'moral' reason. It does not matter much how it is labelled; the point is that it is a *relevant* reason.

If it is objected to my example that I am confusing an official with a personal relationship, my answer is that I am not 'confusing' them but am deliberately ignoring the distinction between them. It is a proper and sometimes an important distinction, but it is not always in place. If we approach this whole matter from the end of the general as opposed to the specific, this distinction would certainly be an important one. That is, if we are looking for an answer to the question, 'Why obey police instructions?' (for, though less general than 'Why obey the government?' this is certainly a general question) we will expect an answer that will make sense in every instance of police instructions, and this requires that we shall not bother about the characteristics of individual policemen or their personal relationships. But if we approach the matter from the end of the specific, and ask 'Why ought I now to refrain from parking by this sign that reads "Police Notice: No Parking"?', we are not bound to give exactly the same kind of answer. As I have insisted, questions expressed in general terms need to be broken down into the specific questions that they are shorthand for if we are not to lose sight of what it is that we are really trying to explain. 'Obedience to government' remains an abstraction unless we are willing to attempt some sort of breakdown of the kind I have been offering

It is perhaps hardly necessary to say that the examples I have given are in themselves of no worth. There are other ways of doing this, and there may well be better ways. What matters is not the examples but the principle that they are intended to illustrate; namely, that in any sphere where human action is involved, a theory must be prepared to stand the test of applicability to *specific* acts. Theories of political obligation are concerned with human action—whatever people do that could be described as obedience to government. A general theory of political obligation, to be acceptable, must cast some light over the whole of this field. The standard theories of political obligation fail to do this. If we start from the end of theory, the problem is to get one's theory to fit plausibly on to all the facts. But why not start from the facts? We may never arrive at a theory, but we may possibly nevertheless come to a better understanding of the facts.

3. The third factor affecting the answer that we might give to 'Why ought we to obey the government?' is that of how the appeal is made. A command of government may come to us with legal sanctions attached; or it may come to us clothed in garments of moral or patriotic hue; or it may come from someone with charismatic qualities; or the appeal may be to our better natures; or arguments of expediency may be used; and so on. There is no need to elaborate. Enough has been said already to show that our judgments about why we ought to obey the government may well be affected by the circumstances—which may be quite various—in which the command of government comes to us.

To sum up the argument of the present chapter, I have tried to show the impossibility of finding a satisfactory, reasonably simple, answer to the question, 'Why ought we to obey the government?'

In the first place, the notion of obedience to government

is really a blanket notion, that must be capable of being applied to a variety of specific types of action, and indeed of specific actions. No single theory of political obligation accounts equally satisfactorily for the whole range of such actions. This I have attempted to establish by considering examples of actions. I have also used the following argument. The standard theories have generally been regarded as rivals to each other. If they are such, then it is likely that no one of them could adequately cover all the ground that all of them together may be supposed to cover. At the same time, however, the advantage that it might seem would be gained by combining the theories into a single complex theory is, I have argued, largely illusory.

In the second place, I have attempted to bring out the fact that the form of words 'Why ought we to obey the government?' is not asking a single, unambiguous question. We need to consider what is meant by 'government', we need to consider what sorts of things may be asked of us, and in what sorts of ways they may be asked. If 'Why ought we to obey the government?' is not a single, unambiguous question we should not expect to be able to give it a single, unambiguous answer.

7

Justifying obligation

I have argued in the previous chapter that theories of political obligation are not adequate to answer the question they are supposed to answer—when that question is broken down into its components. In the present chapter I raise a difficulty of an altogether more serious kind. Can it be not merely that they do badly the task they are designed to do but that the task itself is incapable of being done at all—that the question they are designed to answer is fundamentally misconceived?

A pointless question?

'Why ought we to obey the government?' may well be a pointless question, or, to put it more kindly, a question which answers itself. To refer to something as 'the government' is sometimes a way of saying that it has authority: this is part of what we mean by 'government'. Now, to hold that some person or some body has authority is to hold that he or it ought to be obeyed. This, again, is part of what we mean by 'authority'; that is, authority as opposed to mere power. On this interpretation of 'government' it would be pointless to ask 'Ought we to obey the government?'; for to call something 'the government' precisely is to imply that it ought to be obeyed. Equally, it would be pointless to ask 'Why ought we to obey the government?'. To ask 'why' here would be rather like asking 'Why ought we to do what we ought to do?'.

That the question does not generally strike people as pointless is probably because of the ambiguity of 'government'. For instance, obeying the government may suggest to us obeying the individuals who make up the government at a certain time. (Then the answer, 'Because they are the government' may settle our doubts about whether those individuals ought to be obeyed.) If, for instance, our political sympathies do not lie with the party which has formed a government, we may experience some stirrings of rebelliousness. It is clear that in such a case, although we may use the word 'government', we are in fact thinking of certain men as individuals or as members of a political party rather than of 'The Government' itself, with its connotation of authority. Or, again, to use rather rusty terminology, we may be concerned about questions of *de facto* and *de jure*. We may ask 'Why ought we to obey "the government"?' with an implication that what calls itself the government has no right to the name. Or, yet again, in speaking of obeying the government we may actually be thinking of some particular instruction by the government. After all, obedience to government needs to be translated into action, and quite specific action at that. Once we are faced with a specific instruction, the question of whether we ought to obey or not becomes a real one. We might express our doubts by saying 'Ought we to obey the government?'; but what we would mean by this is, 'Ought we to do such-and-such an act that we are directed to do?', and this might well be sufficiently answered (on one level) by 'Yes; *the government* requires it'. Whether we actually do it or not is another matter; but there is a sense in which there is no doubt that we *ought* to do it.

What is basically the same point can also be argued as follows. Consider the fundamental distinction between anarchy and order. If asked to choose (theoretically) between anarchy and order, we are pretty well bound to choose order. Having so chosen, we have then to choose between different kinds of order. There is, for example, the order of the solitary life, or of the family, or of the tribe. There is the order of the modern liberal democratic State, or of totalitarianism. Each of these can be further subdivided. And so we might go on, listing different kinds and levels of order. Some of them would be mutually exclusive, some not.

Now, about each of these different kinds and levels of order, it may be supposed, questions of the 'why' variety can be asked. Why choose order rather than anarchy? Why choose liberal democracy rather than totalitarianism? Why, having chosen liberal democracy, choose to obey the Prime Minister rather than the Leader of the Opposition? But this last question is at once odd. Having chosen liberal democracy of the modern British kind there is no longer any question of whether we ought to obey the Prime Minister or the Leader of the Opposition. Part of what is involved in choosing the present British political system is precisely that one accepts that the rightful government for the time being has authority, that it ought to be obeyed. If anyone who has so chosen should ask, 'But why ought we to obey the government?', he would only be showing himself up as insufficiently clear-headed. Recognition of the right of a properly constituted British government to require if necessary the obedience of the people is something so fundamental that a man cannot opt out of it without opting out of the British political system. As I have said already. whether he in practice actually obeys the government is an entirely different matter. He can please himself about this. What he cannot please himself about is whether to acknowledge that the government has in general a right to be obeyed, that it ought to be obeyed.

If the reasoning so far presented in this chapter is correct then attempts to construct general theories of political obligation have been fairly decisively disposed of. On the other hand, it is natural to have certain misgivings.

This may seem a suspiciously easy way of disposing of general theories of political obligation. It rests upon an isolation of a certain aspect of the concept of government. If we understand 'government' to mean 'that which has (political) authority in the State' then it follows that if someone is a citizen of a given State he ought to obey the government of that State. This is a very large part of what is meant by being a citizen of a State. But it may well seem to be not much more than a verbal solution to the problem. It is too true to be good. The difficulties about obedience that face people in real life are not met by this solution. Of course, we know that as citizens we ought to obey a body of men that has political authority over us; for we ought to obey those whom we ought to obey. (We ought to do what we ought to do.) But this doctrine may seem too purely formal to be of much use. Certainly, we ought to do what we ought to do. But *what* is it that we ought to do? We must descend to details if we are to meet people's real difficulties about loyalty or rebellion. 'We ought to obey the government because the government is what we ought to obey' is too easy an answer to the question 'Why ought we to obey the government?'.

There is a further objection. This attack on the idea of a general theory of political obligation is conducted too accommodatingly on ground of the enemy's choosing. The terminology used on both sides is one of 'oughts' and 'rights' (and 'orders' and 'obedience'). As I have remarked already, what is needed in discussion of this whole question is an approach not already determined to see the problem in only one kind of light—that shed by the notion of 'obligation'. However, there are times when it is expedient to fight on the enemy's ground, or with weapons of his choice; and, anyway, one cannot be forever questioning the same things. I shall, accordingly, continue the discussion without further complaint about this terminology.

Does the line of argument that I have been developing in this chapter indeed offer no more than a verbal victory? I do not believe so. We shall now see why.

Obligation and society

As we noted in Chapter 5, political obligation is an important concept for certain theorists only—in general, liberals, individualists, believers in the artificiality of society. For theorists of what we may broadly call the Lockean type the concept of political obligation, and questions about the grounds of political obligation, have seemed central. Our discussion has itself looked at the matter— though critically—more or less entirely from within the Lockean standpoint. We have noted particular shortcomings, we have questioned the adequacy of theories; but we have not, in previous chapters, questioned the (unspoken) assumption that if a certain problem exists chiefly for a particular group of thinkers then to understand that problem and its solutions (whether one finds those solutions adequate or not) it is necessary to look at them from the viewpoint of that group of thinkers. But this assumption cannot go unquestioned for ever. When there seems to be no final solution to a problem what is sometimes needed is to look at the whole matter from a quite different point of view. Then what may well happen is not that the final solution so long awaited does at last miraculously appear but that the problem itself vanishes. We have gone as far as we can on Lockean assumptions. The time has come to step out of the Lockean charmed circle.

The question whether society is natural or artificial is an unreal one. The point is that we do live in society, however we may suppose this to have come about. Belonging in society involves the acceptance of rules, and it involves rights and obligations. Understanding what it is to be social would be impossible unless we understood what it is to have rights and obligations—and *vice versa*. (It would be impossible for a man who had accepted membership of a golf club not to accept its rules. Membership of such an association essentially involves rules and obligations; a man who does not see that membership involves obligations is a man who has simply not understood what being a member *means*.) Having obligations is inseparable from being a social creature. The concept of obligation is required in any proper account of the concept of society.

That social man has obligations is therefore not an empirical fact (which might have been otherwise) that calls for explanation or 'justification'. That social man has obligations is an analytic, not a synthetic, proposition. Thus any general question of the form 'Why should we accept obligations?' is misconceived. 'Why should I (a member) accept the rules of the club?' is an absurd question. Accepting the rules is part of what it *means* to be a member. Similarly, 'Why should I obey the government?' is an absurd question. We have not understood what it *means* to be a member of political society if we suppose that political obligation is something that we might not have had and that therefore needs to be *justified*.

But, of course, *specific* obligations may need to be justified. We may (as we have noted in earlier chapters) be legitimately in doubt about whether some specific 'command' of government ought to be 'obeyed'—and for a variety of reasons. But what it does not make sense to ask for a justification of is the existence of *obligations in general*, for that we are involved in obligations is analytically implied by membership of society or societies. We may dispute the secretary's interpretation of some specific obligation but we cannot (logically cannot) dispute that belonging to a club involves us in obligations. We may wonder whether the government is right to require this or that thing of us, but we cannot (logically cannot) dispute that membership of political society involves obligations to government.

To seek a general justification of political obligation—a justification of our being obliged at all in political society —is to pursue a meaningless question. It is to mistake something which is analytically connected with the concept of political society for something which is a purely empirical fact about political societies. The notions of contract, consent, divine right, tradition, etc., have been introduced by theorists in the hope that they will explain or justify something which in reality needs no justification. It is not surprising that we have found shortcomings in the theories built up around such notions. The Lockean approach, we may conclude, is mistaken. In its stress upon the individual and the individual's rights (in many respects admirable) it bases itself on a faulty analysis of the concept of society. The individual, individual rights, and the obligations of individuals, can only be understood in relation to society, not in abstraction from it.

8

Kinds of obligation

It is sometimes held that political obligation is to be simply identified with moral obligation. Sometimes, less simply, it is held that there are a number of completely different kinds of obligation, of which political obligation is only one. In this chapter I consider both these views. It is necessary for this purpose to look at the concept of *obligation* itself, which has been used constantly in this book but has not hitherto been examined.

The concept of obligation

1. 'Obligation', though in origin a legal term, has come to have chiefly a *moral* connotation. This being so, the effect of using expressions like 'political obligation' or 'religious obligation' is undoubtedly to call attention, whether deliberately or not, to respects in which situations referred to by these names are like typical situations of *moral* obligation. Some discussions of political obligation seem to assume almost without question that political obligation must be some aspect of moral obligation. In the question, 'Why ought we to obey the government?', the 'ought' is taken immediately as a moral 'ought'. The extent to which 'ought', 'obligation', and related words have been annexed

66

to ethics makes this understandable if not entirely excusable.

2. 'Obligation' is a relational term. It is used (*a*) of a relation, or one of a number of relations, between individual persons (call them *A* and *B*). One is 'under an obligation to' someone else. People are—or used to be—'greatly obliged to' one another. It is used (*b*) of a relation between a person and an institution, such as the government or a religious organisation (call this a relation between *A* and *I*).

3. Sometimes the relation of obligation is one where something is *owed* by *A* to *B*, or by *A* to *I*. To be under an obligation to someone may be to owe him money, or a service, or one's loyalty, etc. People of independent natures do not like to be 'obliged' to anyone, do not like to feel 'in their debt', to 'owe' them anything.

Owing money—or supposing oneself to owe money—is the most obvious kind of owing. But the ways in which one person may be, or may feel, indebted to another are numerous. Some debts are of a highly informal kind, non-quantifiable, non-enforceable by law; others the reverse. In some cases it is possible both to feel and to be in debt; in others it is all a matter of feeling—but not less real for that. In some cases where *A* owes something to *B* or to *I* it is proper to say that *B* or *I* have corresponding *rights* over *A*; in other cases it would not be proper to say this.

This last point is particularly important. In the case of many (though not all) moral obligations it would be improper to assign corresponding rights. *A* may feel under a deep sense of obligation to *B*, who has saved his life. But there is no question of *B*'s exacting payment for this from *A*, or of his having any consequential rights over *A*. (We should morally approve of *A*'s considering himself obliged to reward *B*. But we should morally disapprove of *B*'s considering that his having saved *A*'s life *entitled* him to some reward from *A*.) It seems, however, that in the case of political obligation it would always be proper to assign corresponding rights. Whenever it is appropriate to say that *A* is obliged to do something that the government requires of him, it is also appropriate to say that the government has a right to his obedience.

4. Sometimes the relation of obligation is better described not in terms of owing something but (as its derivation suggests) in terms of being *bound*. We may be bound to perform some action without in any obvious sense owing anybody anything. This is a sense of obligation perhaps more readily applicable to legal or political obligation than to moral, which is not surprising as it is a survival of the Roman legal sense of the word. This is a metaphor; we are not literally in bonds: but enough of the literal meaning still clings to it to make it not entirely appropriate in a purely moral context. Philosophers, in their analyses of 'obligation', have more to say about 'ought' (which is a form of the verb 'to owe') than about being 'bound'. Yet we express obligations by means of the latter as well as the former.

The metaphor of binding suggests restriction. To be under an obligation in this sense is to have lost a certain amount of freedom, and that freedom is not regained until the obligation has been discharged. Restriction or loss of freedom is not a notion that we generally associate with morality. Admittedly, there are exceptions. Some situations of moral obligation seem to call for expression in the language of *bonds*. But they are, I think, in a minority. Yet in the case of political obligation it seems that freedom is either dispensable with or even sometimes actually inconsistent with it. Certainly, it is not necessary that someone be not under duress for him to be politically obliged : political obligations exist in Police States as well as in liberal democracies. Indeed, if a man's freedom were not somehow being curtailed he would no doubt not be politically (or legally) obliged at all. A legal or political obligation is something that can hurt; ideally, a moral obligation does not hurt : this is as true as most generalisations.

5. There are obligations of which we are conscious and obligations of which we are not. This was hinted at in the distinction mentioned earlier between being in debt and feeling in debt. If a man is obliged by law to pay taxes the obligation is no less real for his being unaware of it. If a man is liable for military service he is no less obliged to accept and act upon the call for his being totally unprepared for its coming. Of course, many of our political and legal obligations we *are* aware of.

How does the matter stand with moral obligations? The obligation on me that may be created by my making a promise does seem to depend in part upon my awareness that I have made it. Suppose I forget that I have made the promise. Am I still under an obligation or not? In a sense, yes; in a sense, no. What is at any rate clear is that there are moral obligations (and promises are an example) that cannot come into existence—whatever may happen to them subsequently—unknown to the persons whose obligations they are. But are there other moral obligations of which this is not true? For instance, is the moral obligation to care for one's parents in their old age one which holds for persons to whom it has never occurred that there is such an obligation? I think we generally so use the expression 'moral obligation' that a man can *not* be said to have a *moral* obligation of which he is not aware. 'Duty' is perhaps a more natural choice if we want a word that is neutral as between the type of case where we are conscious of obligation and the type of case where we are not. Perhaps 'obligation' itself is better reserved for the former type of case only. I do not myself think that there is a completely clear difference of this kind between 'duty' and 'obligation', but the distinction can nevertheless be a useful one.

What is called political obligation does not necessarily

69

depend upon knowledge of its existence. If, by contrast, there is something strained about the notion of a man having a *moral* obligation of which he is not aware, we have here uncovered another difference between political obligation and moral obligation.

6. It seems that obligations may be voluntarily assumed, or otherwise. Again, the examples of promise-making and of liability to tax respectively will serve as examples.

The situation here is parallel to that just discussed under 5. We should, I think, generally be reluctant to use the expression 'moral obligation' for a duty not voluntarily assumed. Some cases covered by the expression 'political obligation' by contrast are certainly cases where we have obligations that we have not voluntarily assumed. Here is again a difference between moral obligations and political obligations.

The upshot of the discussion so far is clear enough. 'Obligation' is understood by philosophers first and foremost as a *moral* term. I have called attention to several points of difference between the concepts of moral obligation and political obligation. We have seen reason therefore to doubt the simple view that political obligation just is moral obligation. I pass now to consider the less simple view that these are different 'kinds' of obligation.

Two kinds of 'kind of'

The existence of *conflicts* of obligation, it is often held, constitutes an important problem, and one that cannot be understood except in terms of different *kinds* of obligation. It is often thought that important conflicts may arise between obligations of different kinds—moral, political, legal, religious—and that the resolution of these may involve serious struggles of conscience. The moral obligation to give help to a friend in financial distress may conflict with the political obligation to pay my taxes. The possibility of conflict between political obligation and legal obligation may seem less real. In Britain today, what the State requires is what the law requires. But in some places and at some times the situation has been otherwise. Conflicts between political and religious obligations are also, it may be said, common enough—in situations where a government is hostile to religion in general or to a particular religious body, or where a religious denomination is opposed to such government policies as compulsory vaccination.

What are we to make of all this? There can be no doubt that the simplest way of describing such situations is as conflicts between different kinds of obligation. But what exactly is meant by the notion of different kinds of obligation? There are two obvious alternatives. *Either* merely that the obligations are 'owed' to people or bodies, etc., to whom we stand in different relationships, and that different sanctions are attached to them, etc. *Or* that there is some different 'quality' of obligatoriness about them. In other words, either we suppose that obligations are obligations, no matter to whom we owe them or how they are enforced (though some may, of course, be more binding than others); or we suppose that not all obligations are just obligations, but that there is some vitally important difference in the 'feel' of them.

Now, the first of these is no doubt innocent enough. We have obligations to parents, to employers, to people to whom we have agreed to sell things, to our country in time of war, and so on. We can for convenience classify our obligations as moral or political or legal, etc., without intending to suggest that there is any difference in 'quality' between them. For instance, some of our obligations are formalised by our having signed a legal document, some are not. There is no harm, and much good, in calling the former legal obligations and the latter something else (nonlegal, perhaps). But the important thing is that although in the sense mentioned—the first of the two senses distinguished above—these are different 'kinds' of obligation, they are not different in the second of the two senses. Obligation is obligation. If we are obliged we are obliged.

The other alternative, however, is not so innocent. This is the notion that the difference between, say, moral obligation and political obligation lies in a systematic ambiguity of 'obligation' itself. The trouble with this is that it is difficult to see how, if this were so, there could ever be legitimate conflicts between (in this sense) different kinds of obligation. How, in this case, would obligations be comparable? What, on this interpretation, would be meant by asking whether a certain religious obligation was more binding than a certain political obligation, or either than a certain moral obligation? If there is to be any kind of conflict at all, at least the contestants must be fighting for the same prize.

It seems that if conflict between different kinds of obligation is to be possible it is necessary that what is meant by 'different kinds of obligation' be merely relatively superficial differences between sub-classes of a single class of things univocally called 'obligation'. If anyone were to insist that there are different kinds of obligation in a more fundamental sense (the second sense, above) this would be at the expense of the possibility of meaningful conflict between different kinds of obligation.

Obligation is obligation. Obligations may conflict, and we may describe such conflicts as being between, say, legal and political and moral obligations; but this way of talking can be somewhat misleading, for what are really in conflict are the obligations, not the legality or politicality or morality of them. Conflict between different *kinds* of obligation is a more theoretically trivial matter than it has been supposed. (It can still be serious practically.) Certainly, it is

72

not the case that the existence of conflict of obligations shows that there are, in the *second* of the senses I have distinguished, importantly different kinds of obligation.

The moralising of politics

Our relationship to government is (at least) one in which we are *required* to do certain things. For philosophers to describe this relationship as one in which we are *obliged* to do those things is (given the predominantly moral overtones of 'obligation') to introduce a moral note—however slight—into the description. That note is appropriate in cases where we actually do—as, of course, we may—feel a moral obligation to comply with what the government requires of us: where, for instance, to repeat a point made earlier, what we are required to do is to pay taxes and we feel moral approval for the purpose for which we are told those taxes are to be used. But not all cases are of this kind.

Some things may be required of us by the government of which we morally disapprove; others of which we morally approve. Is it appropriate to say indifferently of both types of case that we feel 'a political obligation'? It might perhaps be a less misleading account if we marked the difference by saying in the first case simply that such-and-such a thing is required of us by the government, and in the second that we feel an obligation to do such-and-such a thing that is required of us by the government. Here we have not used the term 'political obligation' at all; in the first case because the moral suggestions of 'obligation' seem inappropriate, and in the second because although the moral suggestions of 'obligation' are appropriate the qualifying of 'obligation' by 'political' adds nothing essential: if we feel obliged, what is really important is that we feel obliged, not that we feel politically obliged.

In the previous chapter we completed discussion of the so-called problem of the *ground* of political obligation—which, as I have pointed out, has probably been the main interest of political obligation theorists. After that there still remained something to be done towards the explication of the concept of political obligation itself. The present chapter and that which follows it are intended to further that explication. We have considered in this chapter the relation between political obligation and moral obligation. I have argued that there are some differences between these notions, so that it is not possible simply to identify them, as there has been some tendency to do. But how deep do the differences go? Obligation, as we saw in the previous chapter, is inseparable from social life. Obligations take various forms—legal, moral, political, religious—but the differences between them are not differences in quality of obligatoriness but are explicable in terms of their objects, whether and how they are formalized, the sanctions attached to them, etc. Obligation is obligation. If there are different kinds of obligation the differences are essentially differences within a genus.

Of these kinds of obligation, moral obligation, it cannot be denied, seems to occupy a special place. Moral obligations on the whole seem to people more important than other obligations (or, it may be: the obligations that seem to people most important are those that they class as moral). The term 'obligation', used without qualification, tends to suggest 'moral obligation'. Hence the question of the relation between moral obligation and one of the others seems a more important question than that of the relation between any two of the others. The very use of the term 'obligation' (and associated terms) suggests that moral matters may be involved. Clearly, there are moral questions about politics, but I believe that philosophers have been altogether too ready to look at political *obligation* from a narrowly moral point of view and have consequently not understood it as well as they might otherwise have done. To the discussion of this we now turn.

9

Politics and morals

No examination of the concept of political obligation can omit some consideration of the relation between (*a*) moral and political behaviour and (*b*) ethics and politics as theoretical disciplines. The relation between moral and political behaviour is apt to strike us as a good deal less close than that between ethics and politics. Ethical philosophers and political philosophers tend to be the same people. Moralists and politicians sometimes are but sometimes rather conspicuously are not.

The moral and the political

Morality, it would commonly be said, is concerned with 'personal relations'. (This is in no sense meant as a *definition* of 'morality'.) Politics is concerned with the State and with our relations to the State and its to us—in the liberal tradition with how to achieve peace and security and our interests, and with how to achieve 'more commodious living'. The Greek philosophers did not distinguish as sharply as we do between morals and politics: man is a social and political animal, and the good life is only to be lived in society and, moreover, in political society. Christianity began to alter these assumptions, by laying its stress more on the worth of the individual and the salvation of the individual soul. With the Renaissance there comes a secularisation of the Christian emphasis. Christianity having made the separation between the individual and society (which could then develop into a separation between the individual and the State), and hence between personal relations (morality) and political life, the way is open for Machiavelli to present politics as based on national interest and power and as an activity in which morality may sometimes have to be dispensed with; morality and religion, indeed, are to be *used* by the ruler.

Since Machiavelli, there has been a tendency to assume a difference between moral and political behaviour. There is plenty of evidence to support what is supposed to be the typical reaction of the non-political man: 'Politics is a dirty business'. Sometimes friends are loyally supported through periods of political adversity; sometimes they are dropped. Election promises are broken by politicians when they gain power. We might condemn such things morally while accepting them as politically expedient. We condemn morally the kind of killing called murder but may accept killing as politically necessary in time of war; and some who approve of judicial hanging do so not on moral grounds but on grounds of social or political expediency. Many who condemned slavery and stealing saw nothing wrong in colonial exploitation. 'Business ethics' is a term often used to refer to behaviour that is not ethical at all—not, that is, in terms of a personal morality. The point that emerges from all of these examples is not necessarily, I think, that our *morality* is confused or hypocritical. Sometimes it is, but there is no need to put such an interpretation on these cases. It is rather that certain kinds of behaviour are looked upon as not falling within the sphere of morality at all. The question as people see it is whether they are politically right or wrong (or legally right or wrong, or right or wrong in a business sense); and this seems to them just a different question from the moral one. (I am not, of course, saying that it is thought inappropriate to make moral judgments *about* political events.)

That is the situation on the level of moral and political behaviour. Yet on the level of theoretical study—of ethical and political philosophy as academic disciplines—the situation is different. Political philosophy is a less popular branch of philosophy than is ethics. Perhaps the reason is that people regard ethics as the more fundamental of the two. Clarity about the principles involved in inter-personal relations, it may be supposed, can be fairly easily transferred to provide illumination of person-State relations. It is not at all obvious that this is true; any more than that the reverse order would be true. No one, however, could fail to notice the close connexions that philosophers make between ethical philosophy and political philosophy—exemplified in the existence of 'Social Philosophy' as a sort of hybrid. But the philosophers in this are not reflecting a parallel degree of closeness on the level of practical moral and political thought and practice.

It is a fact that men live in society. In order for this life to be even possible it is necessary that there should be rules or principles of the kind we call moral, legal, political. Our view of the relation between moral rules and political rules will depend (among other things) upon whether we think of organised political society as wholly dependent on the will of man ('the *device* of government') or as a natural outgrowth of man's social existence. If we take the former view (as did Hobbes, for instance) then political rules are likely to strike us as being different from moral rules. If we take the latter view (as did the Greeks) then they are likely to strike us as being basically just moral rules—or, perhaps, moral rules may strike us as being basically just political rules.

Moral principles cannot be deliberately created or terminated by men. If organised political society is thought of chiefly as something set up by the decisions of men, or at least as alterable in various ways by the decisions of men, then political rules or principles will be apt to strike us as being by contrast capable of being created or terminated by men. On the other hand, if we begin from the view of organised political society as some kind of natural outgrowth, it is clear that we are much less likely to see political rules or principles as fundamentally different from moral rules or principles. They are simply the rules or principles that men naturally live by in organised political society, or that they think they ought to live by.

This difference must not be pressed too far. That political society is a natural outgrowth of man's social existence (however precisely we may interpret this) is not incompatible with its being alterable by men's wills. That political society is alterable in various ways by the decisions of men is, indeed, a *fact* about political society. And as there is no sharp line between being 'alterable by' and being 'set up by' men's decisions, it is hard to draw a sharp line between being a natural outgrowth of man's social existence and being set up by the decisions of men. Nevertheless, this distinction does point to an important difference in attitude, and a man's attitude on this goes a long way to determining his views about the relation between moral rules and political rules.

Politics not a branch of ethics

The spectacles through which political philosophers usually look nowadays are such as to show them political principles in the light of moral principles. (This does not mean, of course, that they have nothing to say about differences between moral and political principles. What I am referring to is a certain tendency to import moral notions into politics.)

Political questions are discussed in the terminology of obligations and ideals. The duties of citizens to the State (political obligation), the duties of the State to its citizens, rights and natural rights, sovereignty (where does authority reside in the State?), the ideals of justice, impartiality, responsibility, equality, consent, freedom, punishment (involving discussion of responsibility and free will)—these are things discussed by political philosophers. When political theorists of the past, such as Machiavelli, Hobbes, or Marx, have seemed to some readers to exclude moral categories or to be ambiguous in their use of them, the political philosopher seizes upon this as something of central importance about these theorists. All of this means looking at politics through the spectacles of ethics. It means what I am calling the moralising of politics. (If it be suggested that it might equally well be called the politicising of ethics my answer is that ethics happens to be regarded nowadays as the senior partner.)

Seeing ethics as fundamental and politics as a branch of ethics is a philosophical fashion. There is nothing in the political relationships that *necessitates* their being discussed in the terminology of morality. Philosophers might be well advised to stop discussing political relationships in too narrowly moral terms; they should be clear about the existence of an alternative. By now, admittedly, it would be extremely difficult to provide a completely neutral, non-morally-loaded, philosophical account of political relationships. They have been seen by philosophers in moral terms for so long. the moral flavour has permeated so thoroughly, that it has gone to form part almost of the very nature of these relationships and not merely of their description.

Our concern, however, is with political obligation, not

(absurdly) with the whole of political theory. The man in the street, it seems to me, does not naturally see his relationship to government in terms of obligation. 'Why *do* we obey the government?' is a question that might perhaps occur to him. 'Why *ought* we?' is less likely to. But to the political philosopher this question can seem to lie at the very centre of his subject. There is perhaps no reason why philosophical interests should be expected always to keep in step with interests among the non-philosophical. Many philosophical questions are of importance even though they might not seem so to people who are not philosophers. But that the moralising of political 'obligation' is untrue to the attitude of the man in the voting box can mean that the philosopher is distorting what he is trying to *explain*. It is also the case, as has been mentioned in a previous chapter, that the moralising of politics is not on the whole true to the practice of governments themselves. 'Do this', or 'This is expedient', is the sense of government commands or pronouncements, rather than 'You ought to do this'.

There is another and more important objection to the moralising of politics. If morality is a matter of personal relations and if 'obligation' chiefly suggests morality, relations of obligation, in what we may call the standard sense, hold between individual persons. Obligations can also, of course, as we noted in the previous chapter, be said to hold between individuals and *institutions* (like the government); but this is not the standard moral sense of 'obligation'. We have noted that theorists about political obligation tend to be individualists. Their being individualists may help to account for their wanting to use the notion of obligation at all in connexion with government, but it ought to have also made them wary of doing this very thing. Hobbes is an exception to this; for if his preference for monarchy is taken into account, his system can be interpreted as providing us with just the relation between subjects as individuals and the sovereign as an individual that fits best the standard sense of obligation.

Political obligation, so called, is obligation towards an institution, almost an abstraction, 'the government'. We have discussed the importance of breaking down the notion of obligation towards (or obedience to) *government* into more limited and more personal terms. Thus broken down, the notion of political obligation would be in a form that would lend itself better to interpretation in moral terms than when left in the form of obligation to an institution or abstraction. It is surprising that philosophers, who have moralised politics, have at the same time made things difficult for themselves by interpreting political obligation on the most general and abstract level rather than on the personal level.

Moral and political principles are both to be understood in terms of man's social existence and the rules involved in social existence. There are differences between them, of course, both formal and material, but this is the likeness behind the differences. The kind of moralising of politics that I am objecting to is the kind engaged in by philosophers who attempt to *subordinate* political principles to moral.

There is one way of linking two things that consists in their being seen as aspects of something more general than themselves. There is another way that consists in one of them being forced into the position of a sub-class of the other, which itself is seen as not needing explanation in terms of anything more general than itself. Philosophers have attempted to explain the part in terms of the part. The relation of politics to ethics is not that politics is a branch of ethics. (Neither, of course, is ethics a branch of politics.) The plain man recognises differences between the moral game and the political game. The philosopher, not unaware of the differences, attempts a reconciliation. He achieves it by interpreting political rules as a sub-class of moral rules, but because his view of morality is itself a narrow one (built up around personal relations as the centre) the effect of this can only be to produce a distorted understanding of political rules.

There would be nothing wrong in talking about political obligation, if this talk were more aseptic than it is. The trouble is caused by a certain tendency among philosophers to take moral rules out of the total social situation, interpret them basically in terms of individuals and their relationships, and annex the primary senses of 'obligation' and related terms to morality. Thereafter, to talk of political *obligation* unavoidably suggests an attempt to force political philosophy into the position of a branch of ethics.

10

Conclusion

We noted in the Introduction that philosophers have differed over the place that they assign to political obligation. To some it is the central concept of political philosophy; to others it is of little interest. Which view ought we to take? The answer will be entirely clear from the whole of what has gone before.

We have noted in the foregoing chapters that the concept of political obligation, together with theories about the grounds of political obligation (and the concept itself is chiefly of interest to the extent that it is involved in such theories), has not in fact been considered an essential part of *all* political philosophies. And, assuming for the moment the point of view of those that do use it, we have seen that if it is to have much meaning it requires to be couched in much more particular and specific terms than are in fact provided. We have seen that it involves the moralising of politics. Most important, we have seen that general theories about the grounds of political obligation depend upon a mistaken analysis of the concept of society and man's life in society.

On the basis of all this we may well feel justified in dispensing with the concept of political obligation.

A political philosophy can be constructed that neither

makes explicit use of this concept nor requires it. Such have been constructed. Certain writers have, it is true, felt bound to use the notion of political obligation, but it is so general a notion as to do little or no useful work, and if interpreted in terms specific enough to be useful it is, I have argued, no longer the satisfyingly general thing that those writers wanted in the first place.

As for the moralising of politics implied in the use of 'obligation', this is far from harmless, either to theory or to practice.

For the proper theoretical understanding of the relation between subject and State it is important to be clear that this relation can be explored (as it is by writers on politics whose interest is of a behaviourist or functionalist kind) without its being moralised; and that within the class of social rules political rules—as the Greeks saw—are not properly to be subsumed under the rules of an individualist morality.

The effects on practice of regarding one's relation to the State too much in terms of 'duty', 'obligation', and the like, are to invite the wrong kind of enthusiasm for possibly doubtful ends and an inappropriate kind of guilt at failure to do one's bit adequately towards achieving them.

Bibliography

AUSTIN, J. L., (1962), *How To Do Things With Words*, Oxford: Clarendon Press.

BENN, S. I. and PETERS, R. S., (1959), *Social Principles and the Democratic State*, London: Allen and Unwin, 297-331.

D'ENTRÈVES, A. P., (1965), 'Obeying Whom', *Political Studies*, xiii 1-14.

GREEN, T. H., (1941), *Lectures on the Principles of Political Obligation*, London: Longmans, Green.

HART, H. L. A., (1961), *The Concept of Law*, Oxford: Clarendon Press.

HUME, DAVID, (1965), *Hume's Ethical Writings*, ed. Alasdair MacIntyre, London: Collier-Macmillan, 255-273.

LOCKE, JOHN, (1965), *Two Treatises of Government*, edited Peter Laslett, London: New English Library.

MACDONALD, MARGARET, (1940-41), 'The Language of Political Theory,' *Proceedings of the Aristotelian Society*, xli 91-112.

OAKESHOTT, MICHAEL, (1962), *Rationalism in Politics*, London: Methuen, 1-36, 111-136, 168-196.

PLAMENATZ, JOHN, (1938), *Consent, Freedom and Political Obligation*, London: Oxford University Press.

PLAMENATZ, JOHN, (1958), *The English Utilitarians*, 2nd ed., Oxford: Blackwell, 145-192.

PRICHARD, H. A., (1949), *Moral Obligation*, Oxford: Clarendon Press, 54-86.

REES, J. C., (1954), 'The Limitations of Political Theory', *Political Studies*, ii 242-257.

WEBER, MAX, (1947), *The Theory of Social and Economic Organization*, translated A. M. Henderson and Talcott Parsons, Glencoe, Illinois: The Free Press.